36

P9-BYV-776

The Mysterious & Unknown

Crop Circles

by Stuart A. Kallen

ReferencePoint Press®

San Diego, CA

©2010 ReferencePoint Press, Inc.

For more information, contact:
ReferencePoint Press, Inc.
PO Box 27779
San Diego, CA 92198
www.ReferencePointPress.com

Picture credits:
Cover: www.temporarytemples.co.uk
iStockphoto.com: 42
Landov: 85
Photos.com: 36
Photoshot: 47
Science Photo Library: 31, 57, 65, 71
© www.temporarytemples.co.uk: 7, 11, 16, 20, 44, 69, 77, 80, 91

Series design and book layout:
Amy Stirnkorb

LIBRARY OF CONGRESS CATALOGING-IN-PUBLICATION DATA

Kallen, Stuart A., 1955-
  Crop circles / by Stuart A Kallen.
    p. cm. -- (The mysterious & unknown series)
  Includes bibliographical references and index.
  ISBN-13: 978-1-60152-103-3 (hardback)
  ISBN-10: 1-60152-103-0 (hardback)
  1. Crop circles--Juvenile literature. I. Title.
  AG243.K3243 2009
  001.94--dc22

                                                      2009034368

CONTENTS

FOREWORD

"Strange is our situation here upon earth."
—Albert Einstein

Since the beginning of recorded history, people have been perplexed, fascinated, and even terrified by events that defy explanation. While science has demystified many of these events, such as volcanic eruptions and lunar eclipses, some remain outside the scope of the provable. Do UFOs exist? Are people abducted by aliens? Can some people see into the future? These questions and many more continue to puzzle, intrigue, and confound despite the enormous advances of modern science and technology.

It is these questions, phenomena, and oddities that Reference-Point Press's *The Mysterious & Unknown* series is committed to exploring. Each volume examines historical and anecdotal evidence as well as the most recent theories surrounding the topic in debate. Fascinating primary source quotes from scientists, experts, and eyewitnesses as well as in-depth sidebars further inform the text. Full-color illustrations and photos add to each book's visual appeal. Finally, source notes, a bibliography, and a thorough index provide further reference and research support. Whether for research or the curious reader, *The Mysterious & Unknown* series is certain to satisfy those fascinated by the unexplained.

INTRODUCTION

Mystery in the Meadows

Anyone who types "crop circles" into an Internet search engine will find over 3 million Web pages that mention the mysterious designs found in meadows. Some say the artful patterns, found in fields of flattened wheat, barley, rye, corn, and other grains, are human-made. Others believe the geometric designs are supernatural marvels created by obscure Earth energies or space aliens. Wherever they come from, crop circles have appeared throughout the world—in sugarcane fields in Mexico, rice paddies in China and Japan, and in cornfields in Nebraska.

The term "crop circles" was coined by British electrical engineer Colin Andrews in the early 1980s. It was originally used to describe simple circular patterns discovered in rural areas of southern England. Since that time the designs have become increasingly complex, but they are still called crop circles. The term is also used for eye-catching patterns that have been observed in ice, snow, sand, and various types of vegetation.

Modern crop circle designs incorporate arches, swirls, triangles,

5

Did You
Know?

Modern crop circle
designs incorporate
arches, swirls,
triangles, squares,
pentagrams,
hexagrams, and
other geometric
patterns.

squares, pentagrams, hexagrams, and other geometric patterns. They appear in shapes such as Celtic crosses, figure eights, seashells, and interlocking patterns that appear to have been designed by extremely skilled artists. Some examples are up to 10 acres (4ha) in size and include over 400 separate circles joined into astoundingly complicated patterns. The designs often appear rapidly, sometimes in a matter of several hours.

Some crop circles are known to be human-made, with designers openly claiming credit for their work. Other patterns defy explanation, but this has not stopped various researchers from offering their views. Some say the circles are created from below by unique magnetic energies that emanate from the center of Earth and pull plants down into bizarre shapes. Others believe the circles were created from above by the gods or space aliens trying to convey mystic messages to humanity. This is based on the concept that some of the designs are pictographs, graphic symbols or pictures that have long been used to represent words or ideas.

Some designs, or glyphs, are said to be missives written in binary code, the digital language of ones and zeroes used by computers. A clear example of this type of crop circle appeared August 15, 2002, in Winchester, Hampshire, England. First the face of an alien appeared in a grid of pixels, or small dots similar to those that form pictures on televisions and computer monitors. The next day a disk appeared next to the face with a series of dots and dashes in binary code with the mystifying message: "Beware the bearers of FALSE gifts & their BROKEN PROMISES. Much PAIN but still time. EELRIJUE. There is GOOD out there. We OPpose DECEPTION. Conduit CLOSING."[1]

While no one has been able to decipher the meaning of "EELRIJUE," some believe that the rest of the message is from

The earliest crop circles were little more than crudely formed circles. Modern crop circles come in elaborate shapes and intricate patterns such as this one found in 2005 in Oxfordshire, England.

extraterrestrials (ETs) who are warning humans about the harmful effects of consumerism on the environment. However, skeptics say this glyph, like the vast majority of crop circles, is a hoax. They believe it was created by anonymous circle makers interested only in perpetuating the idea that the patterns are supernatural in origin. As Michael Shermer, editor of *Skeptic* magazine states, "[Even] crop circle enthusiasts and believers admit that 99 percent of all crop circles are man-made hoaxes, what are the odds that the other 1 percent represent something extraterrestrial? Before we say something is out of this world, we need to first make sure that it is not in this world. Crop circles are indubitably this worldly."[2]

Nevertheless, crop circle stories remain popular with the public. In recent years several films, including *Signs* and *Scary Movie 3*, featured crop circles as central story elements. The circles have also been studied in dozens of documentary films and television shows. Despite the attention, crop circle origins remain among the world's leading unsolved mysteries. Like ghosts, UFOs, and other puzzling phenomena, the patterns attract both skeptics and true believers. But whether they are hoaxes or messages from the gods or space aliens, the sheer beauty and complexity of some crop circles is unique among the world's art. Wherever they come from, crop circles add a sense of mystery and magic to otherwise unremarkable fields of grass and grain.

CHAPTER 1

Rings of Record

On June 3, 2009, people in Yatesbury, a small village in Wiltshire, England, discovered an amazing crop circle in a local barley field. The design was in the shape of a huge dragonfly, 150 feet (45.7m) long. The crop circle appeared only days after a gigantic jellyfish pattern, 600 feet (183m) long, was found in nearby Oxfordshire. Commenting on the formation, which resembled a Portuguese man-of-war jellyfish, crop circle researcher Karen Alexander said: "This is the first jellyfish crop circle in the world. It is absolutely huge—roughly three times the size of most crop patterns."[3]

The 2009 crop circle season was extremely busy in Wiltshire, a county in southern England. It began early, in April, and by the time the jellyfish appeared, over 20 formations had been discovered. Many of the patterns were in animal shapes. This led crop circle researchers, or cereologists, to believe that unknown forces were creating the patterns to warn people about the threat of climate change. Alexander's husband Steve, who is a crop circle photographer, comments on this theory:

> Some years you do get themes developing and often you are looking for why this happens. [The patterns could] reflect the status of the world at the moment with its financial, political and more importantly, environmental problems. I imagine this will not be the last [animal pattern] we will see this summer and it has already been a busy summer for spotting them. . . . People believe they will increase in frequency . . . [when] there will be some kind of cataclysmic world event.[4]

The Mowing-Devil

The Alexanders have been dedicated crop circle researchers since the 1970s. They began looking into the strange phenomena when crop circles started to appear with stunning regularity in what is called the Wessex Triangle in Wiltshire, Hampshire, and Sussex counties in southern England. Since the 1970s an estimated 10,000 unusual crop formations have materialized. While 90 percent of the crop circles appeared in southern England, they have also appeared in at least 40 other countries. This has led some to believe that crop circles are a recent phenomenon. However, one of the earliest circles on record can be traced to the seventeenth century.

The report of an ancient crop pattern was described in a pam-

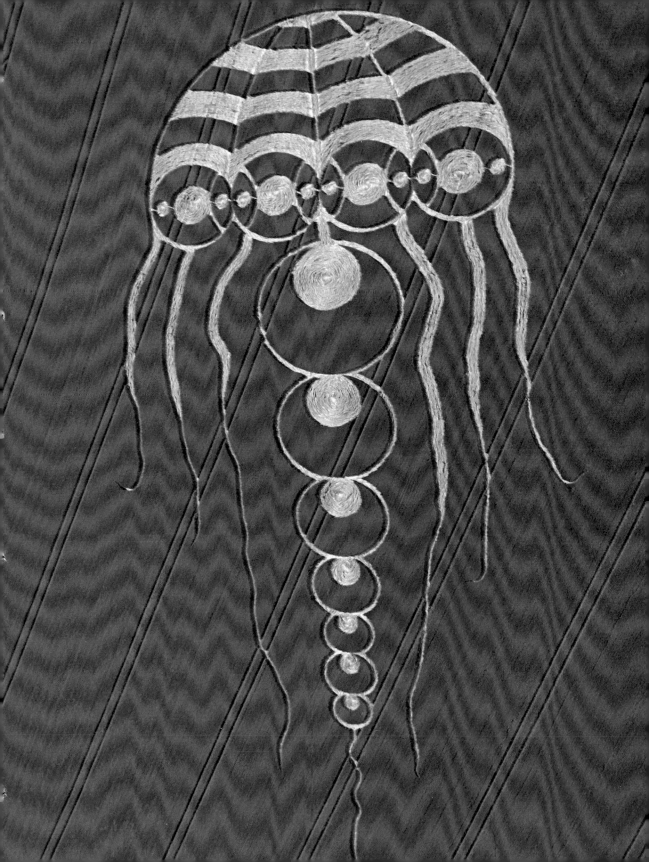

phlet called *The Mowing-Devil; Or, Strange News out of Hart-ford-Shire* that circulated in southern England. The pamphlet contains what is supposedly an eyewitness account from August 22, 1678. *The Mowing-Devil* describes a wealthy farmer in Hert-fordshire who tried to hire a neighbor to mow his oat field. The neighbor asked a high price for his labor, and a heated argument ensued. Finally, according to the pamphlet writer, the exasperated farmer said, "He would rather the Devil himself should Mow his Oats before he would have anything to do" with his greedy neighbor. That night, the sky over the oat field was, as the pamphlet writer noted, "all aflame"[5] with strange lights, leading the farmer and several witnesses to believe the field was on fire.

In the morning, according to the pamphlet, the farmer found: "[The] crop was cut down ready to his hands, as if the Devil had a mind to shew [show] his dexterity in the art of husbandry, and scorn'd to mow them after the usual manner, he cut them in round circles, and plac't [placed] every straw with that exactness that it would have taken . . . an age for any man to perform what he did in that one night."[6] The pamphlet contains a crude woodcut print illustrating the incident. It shows the silhouette of the devil, working with a scythe to create what looks remarkably like a modern crop circle. *The Mowing-Devil* is similar to other pamphlets printed at the time and meant to warn people about the dangers of invoking the devil's name. But modern crop circle enthusiasts have used *The Mowing-Devil* to back up their claims that crop circles are ancient phenomena. They say the description of the strange flaming lights over the oat field bring to mind bright orbs of light that have often been reported over crop circles in recent years. Not everyone agrees with this assessment, however. Skeptics believe that the devil in the picture is simply harvesting the oats, not creating a crop circle.

A Shimmering Rainbow of Light

Perhaps because of their association with the devil, crop circles were rarely spoken of until they began to appear with some regularity in the 1970s. However, in the early 1980s, researchers at Southern Circular Research (SCR) in Sussex began questioning people about crop circle experiences and made some surprising discoveries. The SCR interviewed people who grew up on farms in the 1920s and 1930s. These older citizens remembered stories their grandparents had told them about seeing crop circles in the nineteenth century. Others spoke from personal experience. One woman described a series of triangles she saw in her father's fields in the early 1900s. A brother and sister said they saw a shimmering rainbow of light in the 1950s in a field by Epsom, Surrey. Soon after, a crop circle appeared.

After examining hundreds of similar interviews, researcher Terry Wilson determined that almost 300 crop circles appeared in southern England between 1900 and 1980. At least 25 of these were seen before the start of World War II in 1939. The first crop circle ever photographed from an airplane appeared in a barley field at Bow Hill near Chichester in 1932.

Crushed Wheat

During World War II, while the Royal Air Force (RAF) was conducting regular air patrols across southern England, few crop circle sightings were reported. And in the postwar years the circles remained rare until the mid-1970s when a spate of pat-

Ninety percent of
all crop circles
have appeared in
southern England,
but the formations
have also been seen
in at least 40 other
countries.

terns began attracting widespread interest in Wiltshire County, the traditional center for circle activity.

The activity began on Starr Hill near Warminster. Starr Hill is an oddly shaped sloping knoll on which stand the ruins of an ancient hill fort built around the fifth century B.C. The fort had long attracted tourists, but by the 1970s the ancient Britons who once defended the hill with swords and axes were largely forgotten as a rash of crop circle sightings were reported in the region. Drawn to the excitement surrounding the activity, newspaper reporter Arthur Shuttlewood set up camp on Starr Hill on the night of August 12, 1972, along with American journalist Bryce Bond.

The 2 men were watching the skies when they saw 2 triangles of bright lights appear. About an hour after the odd sighting, the men heard a warbling cricket-like noise, followed by the sound of crushing wheat. According to Bond: "The moon had just come out, shining very brightly and there, before my eyes, a large depression was being formed. . . . The wheat was being crushed down in a counter clockwise position."[7] Shuttlewood later wrote that he watched "an imprint take shape, a large circular area of plants that collapsed like a lady opening a fan."[8] The crushed wheat formed a simple round circle about 30 feet (9.1m) in diameter.

Cosmic Intelligence

The events witnessed by Bond and Sherwood marked the beginning of a very busy decade for crop circles. And as the number of sightings multiplied, so too did the complexity of their designs. In 1978 the first patterns of five circles appeared near Headbourne Worthy, Hampshire. Called quintuplets, or quincunxes, these formations consisted of one large circle surrounded by four smaller satellites, with each smaller circle aligned to the north, south, east, and west points on a compass. This type of complex geometric pattern, discovered and photographed by farmer Ian Stevenson, had never been reported before. However, in the following years quintuplets would become the most common crop circle pattern. And as paranormal researcher Andy Thomas writes in *Vital Signs*, the shapes inspired some cosmic theories concerning their origins: "[The] superficial resemblance of this configuration to the landing pads of NASA lunar craft gave rise . . . to the notion that some kind of cosmic intelligence might be involved."[9]

The increasingly complex patterns found in the fields set off a growing wave of interest in crop circles among scientists, paranormal investigators, and those who study UFOs, called ufologists. Terence Meaden, a meteorological physicist, was one of the early investigators and one of the few with a respected scientific background. In 1974 Meaden was a founding member of the Tornado and Storm Research Organization, which was dedicated to studying rare or extreme weather events. As an experienced atmospheric investigator in Great Britain, Meaden became very interested in crop circles. Between the late 1970s and the early 1990s he visited almost every British crop circle that was reported.

Meaden developed a theory that formations in the fields were created by small localized whirlwinds that touched down briefly to flatten crops. These winds, unlike tornadoes, were stationary. They did not jump around from place to place but remained in one small area. However, many crop circle enthusiasts were not

Many remarkable crop circle designs have decorated the ancient landscape of Wiltshire in southwest England. Dozens of circles, large and small, appeared in this field on Wiltshire's Milk Hill in 2001.

impressed with the theory since whirlwinds rip plants out of the ground and blow them into the sky in a chaotic manner. Discussing crop circles that Meaden had investigated on his land, a farmer named Cooper contradicted the whirlwind theory: "It certainly can't be wind or rain damage because I have seen plenty of that, and [it] is just not that regular."[10]

Multiple Quintuplets

While Meaden tried to explain crop circles with scientific theories, Pat Delgado believed the circles were the workings of "an unknown intelligence."[11] Delgado was a retired electromechanical engineer in Hampshire when his life was changed by a visit to a crop circle site at Cheesefoot Head, several miles outside Winchester. Popular with tourists and hikers, the oddly named Cheesefoot Head is a scenic location that includes a natural amphitheater called Devil's Punchbowl.

Delgado heard about crop circles forming on the night of August 19, 1981, and traveled to Cheesefoot Head the next day. He observed three separate circles sharply cut into the wheat growing in the Devil's Punchbowl. One circle was 51 feet (15.5m) in diameter, while the other two were half that size at 25.5 feet (7.7m) across. The wheat was flattened in a clockwise pattern, and the circle centers were perfectly aligned. The wheat around that formation was not disturbed in any way, and the three impressions were not connected by what are called "tram lines," or parallel tire tracks, made by tractors in the fields. As Ralph Noyes, founding member of the Centre for Crop Circle Studies, writes in *The Crop Circle Enigma*, "There was every appearance that a single event had taken place even if it happened to have had three separate components. "[12]

The precise cut of the circles and the pristine condition of the wheat around them convinced Delgado that they could only have been made from above. Delgado decided to spend his retirement investigating crop circles. He began searching old newspapers and magazines for crop circle reports and contacted the British media when new formations were discovered.

Delgado joined forces with electrical engineer Colin Andrews to form a circle-spotting group whose members included expert ufologist Don Tuersly and a local pilot named Frederick "Busty" Taylor. Together the men began making regular flights around Hampshire in search of new crop circles. When they found a pattern, they would measure it, take photos, and make note of unusual swirl patterns and other oddities.

Although 1982 was a quiet year for crop circles, 1983 was filled with news of many quintuplets, or fivers, sprouting in fields across Wessex. A fiver was discovered at Cheesefoot Head in almost the exact same place as the 1981 circle. Soon more were discovered beneath the ancient hill fort in Bratton, at a site near Clay Hill in Wantage, and even in Vienne in southern France. This new wave of circles quickly grabbed the attention of the British media, as Noyes writes: "Quintuplets caught the imagination of the national media. Articles came thick and fast. Television producers began to take an interest. 1980 had seen the start of scientific attention to the crop circle enigma; 1983 was the year when the British public became aware that something extraordinary was going on."[3]

Humans at Work

The media publicity attracted a new type of circle enthusiast, the hoaxer. Not long after the Bratton fiver appeared, another nearly identical circle appeared nearby. Ian Mrzyglod, a "sky watcher," or someone who scans the skies for UFOs, decided to investigate this new formation. Mrzyglod believed that over 90 percent of flying saucer reports were hoaxes, and he had a skeptical attitude when he began investigating the second Bratton circle. Mrzyglod quickly discovered that a local farmer, Francis Shepherd, admitted using heavy chains to form the crude circles. To make each ring, one of his sons would stand in the middle holding the chain down while Shepherd dragged it around low to the ground. Under further questioning, Shepherd revealed he had been paid by the tabloid newspaper the *Daily Mirror* to duplicate the quintuplet found earlier. The editors at the newspaper were motivated to create their own crop circle because they had been scooped on the first Bratton ring by their competitors at the *Daily Express.*

Nonbelievers assumed Shepherd's methods were used to make most crop circles. However, unlike the first Bratton circle, the farmer's circle was seriously flawed. It was surrounded by a thin outer ring of footprints made by the hoaxers as they dragged a chain to flatten the wheat. And the plants inside the circle were broken and twisted. This was clearly different from the original circle which was cut with precision and filled with bent, not broken, plants. Despite the obvious differences between the two, even Mrzyglod began to doubt the authenticity of crop circles. As Jim Schnabel writes in *Round in Circles*, "If humans had made some of them, then humans could have made all of them."[14]

Jellylike Goo
Crop circle publicity did more than attract the occasional hoaxer. As the number of circles continued to multiply in 1984 and 1985, hundreds of amateur researchers began traipsing the English

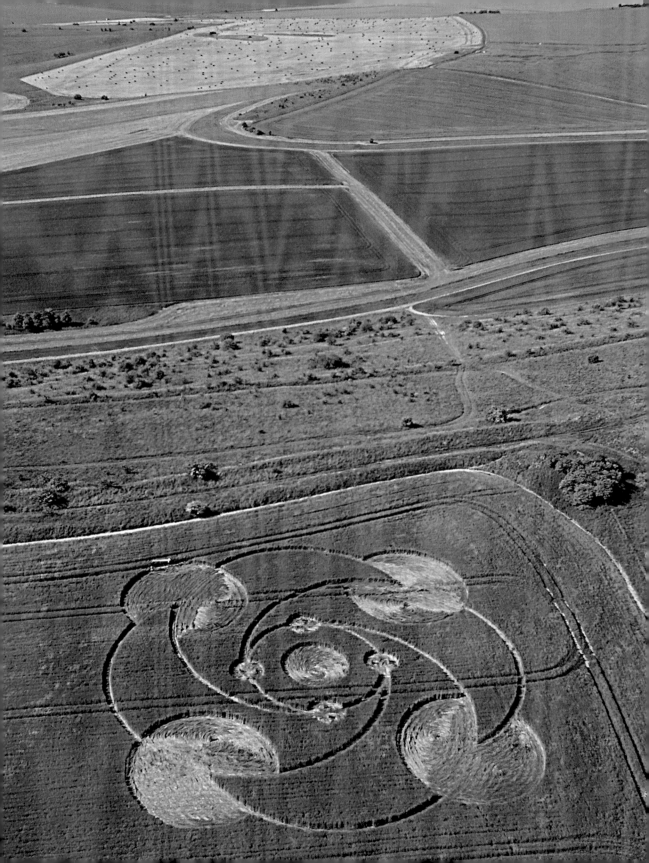

countryside inventing their own theories for the formations. Some said they announced the second coming of Jesus. Others traced crop circles to little green aliens in space ships. Then, the mystery deepened when a new element was added to the crop circle phenomenon.

In June 1985 Taylor was flying over a wheat field in Andover, Hampshire, when he saw a quintuplet. He later told the *Andover Advertiser* the circles were "so neat that it looks as though something has punched them out of the [wheat]." Then Taylor, who had photographed hundreds of crop circles added, "I've never seen anything like it before."[15] After Taylor photographed and videotaped the circle from above, he drove to the location and entered the formation. Taylor felt an unearthly presence, and when he looked at the ground in the main circle he saw a white, jellylike goo on the bent wheat stalks. As he studied the odd substance, Taylor became ill, saying "It gave me stinging sinuses, and eyes . . . . I also suffered a terrific head cold within a matter of hours. . . . It was one of the worst head colds I've ever head in my life."[16]

Before he was stricken, Taylor gathered some of the goo and took it to two agricultural laboratories. One said the jellylike substance contained starch and honey and concluded that it might have been some sort of candy or cake frosting that had seriously spoiled. The other lab noted the goo contained coliform bacteria, commonly found in feces, but the results were inconclusive. Taylor believed that the substance was extraterrestrial in nature.

Operation White Crow

In 1989 Delgado and Andrews published *Circular Evidence.* The authors conclude that "the circles are created by an unknown field force manipulated by an unknown intelligence."[17] *Circular*

Opposite: Quintuplets, crop circle formations that feature a central circle surrounded by four other circles, began appearing in England in the 1970s. A more complex version of the basic quintuplet (pictured) was spotted in 2009 on Knoll Down in Wiltshire.

Evidence eventually sold hundreds of thousands of copies and popularized crop circles throughout the world. As best-selling authors, Delgado and Andrews were elevated to the role of crop circle experts by print and television reporters. Meaden published his own book, *The Circle Effect and Its Mysteries*, around the same time. Unlike Delgado and Andrews, Meaden surmised the circles were formed by wind and weather patterns. Meaden's book, which was based on scientific principles, was largely ignored by the media.

Taking advantage of their new celebrity, in June 1989 Delgado and Andrews set up the world's first crop circle surveillance program, Operation White Crow. The goal of the program was to capture a video of a crop circle being formed and thereby prove that supernatural intelligence was behind the phenomenon. Operation White Crow lasted for eight days and nights. During the event 60 people, working in 4-person shifts, kept round-the-clock surveillance over Devil's Punchbowl. They operated from a small truck equipped with specialized low-light and image-intensifier cameras. During the extensive operation, no one observed a crop circle being made, although several appeared in nearby locations. However, sky watchers did report seeing unusual lights at night.

The most unusual event during Operation White Crow occurred on June 18, the last night. Six observers were sitting in an old crop circle when they heard a piercing sound. Andrews captured the sound on his tape recorder. Skeptics claim the sound came from a small bird called the grasshopper warbler, but this bird is not native to the area. When the tape was analyzed by NASA's Jet Propulsion Laboratory in California, audio scientist Robert Weiss could not identify the noise. He did determine, however, that it was artificial in origin and not made by a living creature.

A Major Turning Point

Operation White Crow received considerable publicity in Great Britain, but it was quickly overshadowed when a new type of crop circle appeared on August 12, 1989. The 60-foot circle (18.2m) was found in a field near Winterbourne Stoke, Wiltshire. This glyph was more complex than any that had been previously observed. In the center, grasses were bending in three different directions, making a swirl of woven plants that was 9 feet (2.7m) across. Around this intricate interwoven pattern, 4 quadrants were formed with the grasses sweeping out in several different directions.

The new design was called the Solar Cross. The unique, complex pattern resembled an ancient symbol seen on burial urns that were made in Great Britain around 1440 B.C. These ancient stone pots had been unearthed by archeologists in Croft, Cheshire, in the early 1980s. Crop circle researchers believed the 4 divisions within the circle, which were aligned with the 4 compass points, represented the 4 seasons.

Whatever the meaning of the Solar Cross, its appearance marked a new phase in crop circle designs. This pattern was clearly not made by stationary whirlwinds and seemed much too complex to have been created by hoaxers. Commenting on this new development, Thomas writes:

> Though few realized it at the time, with this event, the game-plan had changed and the mystery was to take a huge leap forward when the stems of the

following season began to push their way upwards. . . . [No one] was prepared for the shapes which began to appear in 1990. Although there is evidence to suggest a small number of complex patterns had appeared before, there's little doubt that this year was the major turning point in the development of the crop circles. It's easy in retrospect, with complicated designs now a familiar sight, to forget the terrific impact of what became known as the 'pictograms.'... To many, these strongly suggested a premeditated source. [18]

A second complex pictogram occurred in a familiar place, Cheesefoot Head, on May 23, 1990. This formation consisted of a large circle attached to a very straight central pathway which led to a smaller circle. On either side of the wide pathway two precise long rectangular boxes, like the number 11, were formed in the field.

About 2 months after the Cheesefoot Head incident, the most complex formation to date appeared near the small village of Alton Barnes, Wiltshire. The crop circle was 606 feet (185m) long, much larger than anything previously seen, and the design consisted of rings, boxes, circles, straight lines, and 3-pronged tridents. It appeared after a night in which loud rumbling sounds were heard in the village, and dogs barked relentlessly. The following morning several fairly new cars in the village could not be started for unknown reasons.

Farm manager Tim Carson discovered the crop circle and notified the press. By noon on July 12 reporters were on the scene. That evening the Alton Barnes crop circle made national news, and within a day the story was picked up by the international media. As the week ended, thousands of tourists, some from as far away as Japan, swarmed the tiny village. In the carnival-like atmosphere, people danced inside the circle and spoke to one another about who or what created the complex pictogram. Officials tried to explain away the phenomenon, blaming it on pranksters. But as crop circle researcher Freddy Silva writes in *Secrets in the Fields*, "Public and media confidence in official explanations evaporated as crop circle fever broke out."[19]

The same night the Alton Barnes crop circle was created, a similar circle appeared in a field about a mile away. Commenting on the appearance of the circle in his field, a farmer, who had been harvesting wheat the day before stated, "It wasn't there when I drove down here last evening, but it appeared here during the night. I cannot think of anything that could do this, can you?"[20]

The Mother of All Crop Circles

During 1990 five similarly complicated designs were discovered around Cheesefoot Head. Some consisted of three circles connected by straight paths, others were adorned with half circles outside the larger rings or swooping lines crossing straight paths. Most incorporated the rectangular 11 pattern. The following year the pictograms continued to evolve. Some looked like dolphins and were referred to as dolphinograms. Circles called insectograms looked like various bugs. Others mimicked computer-generated motifs called fractals. These were called Mandelbrot sets after Benôit Mandelbrot, the mathematician known as the father of fractal geometry.

On July 17, 1991, what was called the mother of all crop circles arrived near the Iron Age hill fort called Barbury Castle, in Wiltshire.

"If humans had
made some of
them, then humans
could have made
all of them."
—Jim Schnabel,
author and crop
circle researcher.

The Miamisburg Crop Circle

Nine of out 10 crop circles are found in southern England, which is also home to the most complex pictograms and geometric forms. Crop circles in the United States tend to be simple in design and most have been shown to be human-made or related to weather conditions. However, on occasion a complex circle of unknown origin does appear in the United States. Perhaps the most mysterious American crop circle appeared in Miamisburg, Ohio, on September 1, 2004. The circle appeared near the Miamisburg Mound, a gigantic, 7-story-high burial mound made by

The design consisted of a large center circle surrounded by three outer rings that occupied 12,000 square yards (10,033 sq m). The circles within the formation were filled with triangles, rings, arches, and straight lines, and the exquisite design features captured public attention. Some said the glyph contained symbols used in

Native Americans about 2,000 years ago.

The Miamisburg crop circle was 222 feet (67.6m) long and appeared in a field of ripe corn 8 feet (2.4m) high. The pattern consisted of a large circle crowned by a smaller circle. Within the circles were shapes that looked like a pair of wings, an eye, and a quarter moon. The corn was flattened in graceful curves, which implies that the stalks were softened by heat. The Miamisburg circle was not visible from the ground and was only discovered when a police helicopter flew over it. Experts determined that because of the way the plants were recovering, the circle was approximately 7 days old at the time of discovery. Like many crop circles found elsewhere, the source of the Miamisburg formation remains unknown.

ancient magic books. Others believed the design was similar to the tree of life found in the teachings of the Jewish Kabbala.

Whatever the meaning behind the Barbury Castle formation, it mainly served to intensify crop circle fever. Thousands of international travelers poured into the English countryside looking for the supernatural circle makers. And as a record number of circle seekers arrived, the formations began to multiply rapidly. Approximately 800 crop circles were created in England in 1991 with 500 in Wiltshire alone. Nearly every one was reported in the media, and the complexity and size of the circles continued to grow.

The early 1990s also saw the number of circles increasing in other countries. A 59-foot circle (18m) appeared on Kyushu Island, Japan, in 1992. The rice farmer who owned the field believed at first that the formation was caused by a wild boar. In Saskatchewan and Manitoba in Canada, circles showed up in dozens of wheat fields. And in the midwestern region of the United States, the arrival of crop circles stirred talk of whirlwinds, tornadoes, hoaxes, and UFOs. However, most crop circles outside of England were crude formations and seemed to be the work of pranksters trying to imitate the glyphs in England.

By the end of the 1990s at least 10,000 crop circles had been reported worldwide. While viewed by millions of people after their creation, at least 80 people said they watched crop circles materialize. These eyewitnesses had similar stories. They said the circles took about 20 seconds to form, and the event was often accompanied by strange bright lights. Sometimes unidentified flying objects were said to shine beams of light on the field the night before the incident.

As the twenty-first century dawned, the mysterious pictograms that first appeared in England had become worldwide phenomena. The Internet was filled with thousands of pictures and eyewitness accounts. Mystics, religious seekers, pranksters, scientists, media producers, and average citizens all weighed in on the meaning and the makers of the designs. While the crop circle craze might have died down if the glyphs stayed the same, some of the English designs looked like pixilated photographs. These were beyond the wildest expectation of cereologists.

Even as public fascination continues to grow, so does widespread disagreement as to who—or what—is creating the formations. Jokesters, winds, UFOs, or all three might be responsible for the weirdness in the wheat. Or perhaps an undiscovered energy is at work. Whatever the source, new circles are cropping up in England and elsewhere in the world on a regular basis. They are beautiful, they are captivating, and they invoke thoughtful discussion among observers. Unlike the evil Mowing-Devil of the seventeenth century, the crop circle phenomenon of the modern age is seen as a positive force. And some believe that is the best way to see the circles, as a welcome respite in a world often filled with negative news.

CHAPTER 2

Earth
Energies

On July 7, 1996, pilot Rod Taylor flew his small airplane 7 times around Stonehenge, a mysterious ring of massive stone pillars in Salisbury, England. Taylor was an experienced pilot who had been observing crop circles from the air since the early 1980s. After passing over Stonehenge at 5:30 P.M., Taylor flew off in search of crop circles elsewhere in Wiltshire County. Thirty minutes later, he returned to Stonehenge and was stunned by what he saw. During his short absence, in broad daylight, an incredibly large and complex crop circle had appeared in the wheat. It consisted of 149 separate circles laid out in a giant

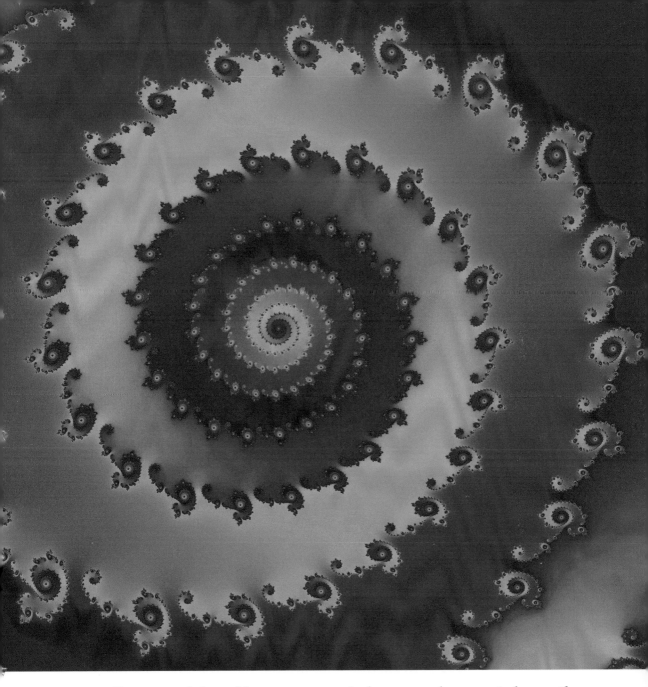

In 1996, a pilot reported the sudden appearance of a large, complex crop circle near the ancient stone monument of Stonehenge. The crop circle resembled a spiral pattern known in mathematics as a Julia Set fractal. A computer-generated example appears here.

Earth Energies

spiral about 500 feet (152.4m) wide and 915 feet (279m) long. The intricate pattern was later named the Julia Set after a shape created with fractal geometry.

The wheat field with the Julia Set was separated from Stonehenge by a very busy highway. A farmworker, crowds of summer tourists, a Stonehenge security guard, and hundreds of people in their cars were in the vicinity. But no one witnessed the circle's creation. It was as if the formation appeared out of thin air.

Ley Lines and Crop Circles

Hours after the Julia Set was spotted, pictures of the astoundingly beautiful formation appeared in newspapers, on television, and on the Internet. The formation attracted intense interest because it was the most complicated glyph seen to date. But the circle's location gave the Julia Set an extra aura of mystery because Stonehenge is one of the most mysterious places in England.

Stonehenge was built around 4,500 years ago, but by whom is uncertain. Its construction has been attributed to the Romans, Greeks, Egyptians, Celts, Druids, and even the legendary magician Merlin. Whoever constructed Stonehenge moved massive rocks that weighed between 5 and 25 tons (4.5–22 metric tons) without the use of cranes, hoists, or machinery. The monument is said to have taken an estimated 30 million worker-hours to build. Researchers have not been able to determine how the stones were stacked so that they accurately align with the summer solstice. But when the sun rises on the longest day of the year, around June 21, its first rays shine between the main group of upright rocks into the center of the monument.

Stonehenge is one of many Stone Age, or Neolithic, monuments in Wiltshire that were built between 4000 and 2000 B.C. Other sites include Silbury Hill, a human-made chalk mound that is 130 feet (40m) high. The West Kennet Long Barrow, a Neolithic tomb, is close to Silbury Hill. A nearby circle of large upright rocks called the Avebury Ring is older than Stonehenge. Crop circles have appeared with astonishing regularity at all of these sites in recent years.

Some believe that henges, barrows, and mounds in England and elsewhere are connected though an invisible energy network called ley lines. These lines supposedly run along the Earth near the surface of the ground. The ley line theory was conceived in 1925 by inventor and natural historian Alfred Watkins. He believed that these unseen lines of energy connect Neolithic sites with natural features such as ponds, springs, underground reservoirs, and lakes.

Ley lines supposedly cross the Earth like an invisible grid. They are most powerful where two ley lines intersect, a place called a ley line vortex. A vortex is a whirlwind of energy that draws everything near it into its center. The plural of vortex is *vortices*, and Watkins believed ancient people built temples and monuments on top of ley line vortices.

In the 1970s, when crop circles began to appear regularly near the Neolithic monuments in the Wessex Triangle, some researchers began to associate crop circles with ley lines. They said that the stored energy under ley line vortices bubbled to the surface like lava from a volcano. This invisible force created crop circles by emitting magnetic energy that pulled plants down into interesting patterns.

Another ley line theory is based on the idea that the vortices

Natural histo-
rian Alfred Watkins
believed England's
prehistoric stone
monuments are
connected by an in-
visible underground
energy source called
ley lines.

meet above underground water reservoirs. This water is drawn to the surface and makes crop circles by emitting steam. Cereolo-gists Judith Moore and Barbara Lamb explain:

> The underground water is necessary for the steam effect that seems to be involved with the making of crop circles. Some crop circle scientists theo-rize that when the heat of 500 degrees Fahren-heit or higher is applied to the plants as abundant moisture is being drawn up from under the soil, the plants become pliable enough to be gently bent over at ground level without any cracking, breaking, or killing, and then to be swirled or shaped to form a variety of patterns.[21]

Moore and Lamb believe that the underground water theory explains why crop circles are more abundant in some years than others. For example, in 1995 England suffered a long drought. As underground water tables fell, fewer crop circles appeared.

The Plasma Vortex Theory

In the field of crop circle study, the ley line theory is only one idea that focuses on vortices. Another is called the plasma vortex theory and is based on the idea that crop circles are created by high-energy whirlwinds as powerful as lightning. This concept can be traced back to 1686 when an Oxford chemistry professor named Robert Plot studied formations he called "Fairy circles." Some were small, around 6 feet (1.8m) in diameter, while others were quite large, up to 120 feet (35.8m) across. Plot wrote that some of the outer rings were not quite perfect circles but ovoid, or egg shaped.

As Plot traveled the English countryside he viewed various crop circle designs that would be familiar to modern researchers. In open, treeless fields the professor saw patterns that consisted of 2 or 3 interwoven rings. He even said he viewed several square patterns, or grid squares, inside of the rings. Some were divided into 4 or 6 segments by lines of unbent vegetation.

In his 1686 book *The Natural History of Staffordshire*, Plot attempted to explain how the fairy rings were formed. He theorized that they were created by an unusual type of lightning that would break through the clouds and hit the ground in a circular pattern. This lightning could occur in a single burst or along with two or three other hits that could create more intricate patterns. To illustrate his theory, Plot drew sketches of lightning "trumpets" that shot out energy to form crop circles.

Plot's lightning trumpets were remarkably similar to the plasma vortices that Terence Meaden attributed to crop circle formation in the 1980s. Meaden defined a plasma vortex as "a spinning mass of air which has accumulated a significant fraction of electrically charged matter."[22] Meaden hypothesized that unusual wind vortices are formed high above the ground when dust and microwave energy interact with electromagnetic charges. This force is similar to the one that produces lightning. In Meaden's theory, the dust particles within the vortex become electrified, or ionized, and produce a powerful electrical charge called plasma. Within the spinning, ionized plasma cloud, dust particles take on an eerie glow. This is said to explain why witnesses often see unearthly lights near crop circles. According to

Meaden, at some point the highly charged plasma vortex suddenly descends to the ground in a moving spiral that gently bends the plants in a field. The stalks show no damage as would be the case if they were hit by a normal tornado or whirlwind.

It is unknown if Meaden based the plasma vortex theory on Plot's lightning trumpets. However, his explanation does not account for the complex geometric patterns and pictograms like the Julia Set. Meaden has a simple answer to critics of his theory. He speculates that large numbers of crop circles, especially the elaborate pictograms, are produced by hoaxers.

Astonishing Anomalies

Meaden's proclamation that pranksters are at work in the fields has been cheered by circle skeptics. However, American biophysicist William C. Levengood was not convinced that humans were making crop circles. Levengood based his findings on plant and soil samples mailed to his Pinelandia Biophysical Laboratory in Grass Lake, Michigan, by Pat Delgado in 1989.

Delgado noted that farmers reported that the dirt within crop circles had an unusual odor but was healthier and had a brighter luster than surrounding soil. When the circle areas were replanted with fresh crops the following year, the plants seemed to grow bigger and faster than others in the field. Plot had noted this in 1686 when he wrote that the soil within crop circles had a "musty rancid smell"[23] similar to moldy bread. In addition, "the earth underneath [was] highly improved with a fat sulpherous matter . . . ever since it was first stricken, though not exerting its fertilizing quality till some time after."[24] Levengood wanted to learn if this was actually the case and, if so, why the soil was different within crop circles.

Knives, tools, and other metal items become magnetized when carried into crop circles.

Levengood used powerful microscopes to examine plants taken from crop circles. He found enlarged holes, called pits, in the cell walls. Cell wall pits allow cells to absorb and excrete matter and fluids. Levengood concluded that the pits were enlarged by a very quick and brief heating process, which forced them to expand. He duplicated this force by placing normal plants in a microwave oven, which exposed them to radiation.

Levengood was amazed by his findings and formed the Burke, Levengood, Talbott (BLT) Research Team in 1992 to continue investigating crop circle plants. Since that time BLT has analyzed plants and soil samples taken from over 300 crop circles worldwide. After comparing the samples with samples taken from outside the formations, team member Nancy Talbott concluded, "Astonishing anomalies were observed in the structure of the material taken from inside the crop circle."[25]

Talbott is the president of the BLT Research Team, carries out fieldwork for the group, and has published over 50 articles in scientific journals. Talbott often writes about the unusual plant anomalies found in crop circles. The plants have longer and thicker nodes, which are places on the stems where leaves are attached. BLT also discovered obvious bending of the nodes at odd angles while some growth nodes burst open completely, as if exploding from within. The seed heads of the plants were deformed, with some seeds missing and others stunted. Some of the plants germinated from these seeds were stunted as well. Others grew faster and were stronger than normal seedlings.

Another mysterious finding involved fields where rapeseed is grown to produce canola oil. Rapeseed plants are as thick and unbendable as celery stalks. If they are bent more than 45 degrees, they break. However, when crop circles appear in rapeseed fields, the unbendable plants are bent flat at 90 degree angles. No one has been able to explain this phenomenon.

Talbott emphasizes that the BLT research was blind; that is, it was conducted without knowing if the plants being examined were from outside or inside a crop circle. The group even conducted blind tests on plants from human-made formations. But plants taken from "genuine" crop circles (those with unexplainable origins) were readily identified by various anomalies, which occurred in at least 95 percent of the samples. According to Talbott, these plants show "evidence of exposure to rapid air movement, unusual electrical fields [and] very brief exposure to extreme heat."[26]

Shooting Stars and Crop Circles

Levengood coined a term for the odd physical occurrences. Because the idea was loosely based on Meaden's plasma vortex theory, it was called the ion-plasma vortex theory. In 1994 Levengood published a scientific research paper describing the ion-plasma vortex. While Meaden believed highly charged plasma vortices pushed plants down into patterns, Levengood stated that microwave energy heated the plants. This caused plant tissues to bend into symmetrical patterns such as circles, rings, triangles, double lines, and ovals. Talbott later discussed the power of the ion-plasma vortex: "Although it is difficult for most people to imagine, it is entirely possible for such vortices to produce an enormous variety of complex geometric patterns upon impact at the Earth's surface."[27] She believes that the specific weather patterns of southern England are most favorable for producing ion-plasma vortices, which is why 90 percent of all crop circles are found there.

A 1993 discovery at a crop circle in Cherhill, England, added

another twist to the ion-plasma vortex theory. Some of the plants found at the very center of the formation were coated with a brown, iron glaze. This was made from fused particles of the minerals hematite and magnetite. The Cherhill formation appeared during the annual Perseid meteor shower. The cosmic shower occurs when the Earth moves through a cloud of meteors that stretch along the orbit of the Swift-Tuttle comet. During the height of the Perseid event, between August 8 and August 14, at least 60 meteors, or shooting stars, can be seen every hour in the Northern Hemisphere.

Levengood believes the microscopic iron particles found in the Cherhill crop formation were meteoric dust. He believes the comet dust filtered into the air as meteors were burning up upon entry into Earth's atmosphere. According to Levengood, the dust was drawn into the ion-plasma vortex by the strong magnetic field within the whirlwind. The microwaves in the plasma heated the meteor particles and fused them into the hematite and magnetite glaze found within the crop circle.

After this discovery, BLT began sampling crop circle soil regularly. The team learned that tiny particles of unusually pure and perfectly round iron often appear inside the rings. Levengood believes much of it is meteoric in origin. These particles are strongly magnetic, and magnetism has long been associated with crop circles. As far back as 1927 it was observed that knives, tools, and other metal items became magnetized when carried into the formations.

Magnetism has also been traced to technical problems people have with electrical equipment inside crop circles. Silva writes that in 2000 his relatively new camera stopped working when he entered a lotus flower formation near Golden Ball Hill. When he took it in for repair he was told that the circuit board in his camera was destroyed. The repair technician added, "We have had a record number of identical problems with cameras this summer, and the strange thing is, their owners all claim the problems happened when they took [the cameras] into crop circles."[28]

Not all electrical problems are as permanent as Silva's. Others have noted that their cell phones stop working in crop circles only to function perfectly when carried out of the formations. Similar stories are told of tractor engines stalling when the machines drive into circles. After being pushed out of the rings, the engines spark back to life. The circles also wreak havoc with batteries. For example, in 2002 a Japanese researcher found that the heavy-duty battery pack for his video camera, with a 14-hour charge, drained instantly when he entered a crop circle. People have had similar problems with watches, laptop computers, and camcorders.

Effects on People and Animals

Living creatures are oddly affected by crop circles, and this has also been blamed on electromagnetic forces within the formations. Observers have noticed that geese break their "V" formation when passing over fresh crop circles, then resume the flying pattern afterward. Red deer have been seen avoiding crop circles that have formed across their usual paths through fields. And domesticated animals often create a ruckus when the circles form in the middle of the night. Dogs will bark relentlessly and cattle will become restless and bellow through the night. It has also been reported that some dogs will become terrified and refuse to enter crop circles.

Bright yellow flowers decorate the stems of rapeseed plants. Though the stems are as thick as celery stalks, crop circles found in rapeseed fields have bent rather than broken plants.

Humans also seem to be affected by crop circle energy, especially when the formations are new. People have reported a host of ailments, including splitting headaches, nausea, dizziness, disorientation, heart palpitations, and feelings of extreme fear. Not all reactions are negative, however. Some say upon entering crop circles they felt peace, joy, love, exuberance, a sense of "oneness" with all people. Commenting on the unusual effects, Talbott writes:

> It is easy, perhaps, to dismiss such reports as being due to some sort of hysteria or over-excitement, and there seems to be no evidence of long-term effect to either people or animals. However, the fact is that a large number of field personnel who have spent considerable time in the formations, as well as some of the more casual visitors, have experienced one or several of these effects in crop circles all over the world. The fact that most of these experiences are reported in newly-formed crop circles suggests there may be a remnant energy still present at some of these sites, to which at least some people are sensitive.[29]

Mind Movement

While theories of comet dust and plasma vortices satisfied some crop circle researchers, others looked inward for explanations. Some focused on the human mind, believing the formations in the fields are created by unconscious human thoughts. This might affect crop circles in several ways. Some believe that the designs may be made by people emitting intense mental energy that affects the physical environment. This concept is referred to

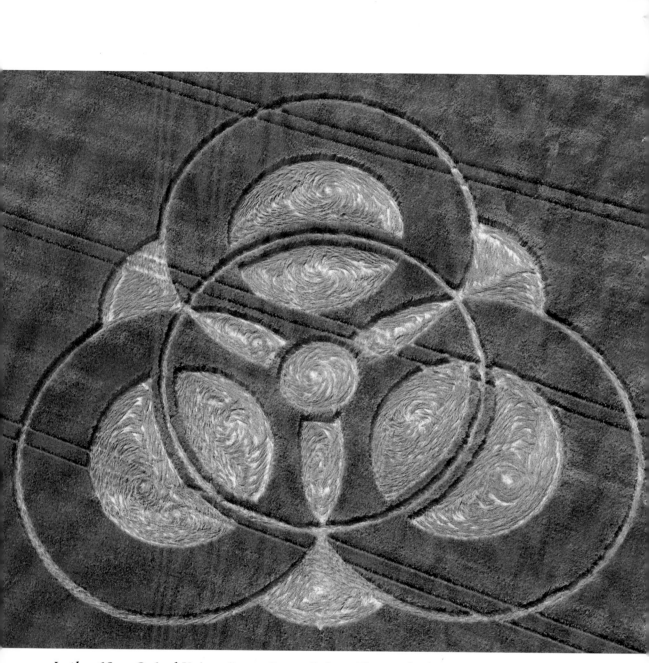

In the 1680s, Oxford University professor Robert Plot studied patterns of interwoven rings scat-tered across the English countryside. They would have looked something like this more elaborate ring pattern, photographed in Wiltshire in June 2009.

as "recurrent spontaneous psychokinesis," or RSPK energy. (The term *psychokinesis*, or "mind movement," is derived from the Greek words *psyche*, or "mind," and *kinein*, "to move.")

By using PK energy, people can allegedly bend spoons, make objects fly around the room, and even manifest gooey slime, called ectoplasm, on walls, ceilings, and floors. While these events are commonly associated with mischievous ghosts called poltergeists, some believe that the ability to bend spoons would also allow people to use PK energy to bend plant stalks. In addition, crop circles that contain slime similar to ectoplasm have been reported many times. To explore the PK energy theory, Talbott traveled to the home of Robbert van den Broeke in Hoeven, Holland, in August 2001.

Van den Broeke first came to the attention of BLT Research in 1996, when he was 16. At that time he reportedly saw strange balls of light and an angel rising out of a fresh crop circle that was discovered in the Hoeven region. After that experience, Van den Broeke began having lucid dreams in which he was able to accurately determine where and when a crop circle was forming in the area. In addition, Van den Broeke began taking photographs of crop circles at night, which revealed light globules hovering above the formations. Since the late 1990s Van den Broeke has become a well-known medium, able to bend forks by directing mental energy through his fingertips. He can also make forks, knives, and spoons stick to his forehead and chest as if he were a large magnet.

New Aspects of Reality

When Talbott arrived to study Van den Broeke's mental energies, she stayed at the farm where he still lived with his parents. She

*Opposite:
One research-
er believes
that cosmic
activity
during the
annual Per-
seid meteor
shower may
be responsi-
ble for certain
crop circle
formations.
Here, two
astronomers
watch as me-
teors streak
through the
night sky dur-
ing the Per-
seid meteor
shower.*

slept in a second-floor bedroom that overlooked a farm field planted with string beans. Her stay had been uneventful, and before she went to bed in the early morning hours of August 21, she complained to Van den Broeke that the trip had been a waste of time because no new crop circles had formed.

Talbott's disappointment ended at 3:15 A.M. when she was awakened by the loud bawling of cows. Talbott jumped from her bed to look out the window of her room. Suddenly everything was illuminated by tubes of light about 1 foot (0.3m) in diameter. The lights were as bright as the searchlights found on helicopters and blasted brilliantly above the bean field, but they lasted only a few seconds. However, second and third tubes soon appeared, both with a bluish tint. A fourth tube spiraled down to the ground as Talbott ran down the stairs to see Van den Broeke peering intently out the kitchen window at the display.

The tubes of light vanished as suddenly as they appeared, and the night returned to normal. Talbott and Van den Broeke ran outside and discovered a fresh crop circle in the bean field. Half the crop in the area was flattened in the direction of the farmhouse and the other half was flattened in the other direction. A faint steam rose from the downed plants which were heavy with beans almost ready to be harvested.

The next day Talbott examined the circle she believes was made by Van den Broeke's mental energy. It was about 35 feet (10.6.m) long and 20 feet (6.1m) wide with a T-shaped, 20-foot-long pathway (6.1m) with a crossbar at the end. That night, photos were taken within the crop circle, and when the film was developed the pictures showed multiple light orbs in the formation, with some about 5 times larger than a soccer ball.

Stoned Wallabies Make Crop Circles

Throughout the centuries, crop circle formations have been attibuted to many types of animals, including mating hedgehogs and wild boars. But in June 2009 a story from the Australian island of Tasmania was unique even among the many wild theories about crop circles. Tasmanian government officials told BBC News that unusual formations were appearing in the island's opium fields. Tasmania is one of the few places where the powerful drug opium is legally grown for medical purposes. The island supplies 50 percent of the world's medicinal opium, which is used to make prescription drugs like morphine as well as heroin. According to the BBC report, wallabies (small kangaroo-like marsupials) were getting into the opium fields, eating the drug, and becoming "high as a kite." Authorities believe that the drugged animals proceeded to run in circles, smashing down the plants into odd patterns.

Quoted in "Stoned Wallabies Make Crop Circles," *BBC News*, June 25, 2009. http://news.bbc.co.uk.

While the Hoeven crop circle was similar to hundreds of others, Talbott believes that mental energies were responsible for its creation:

> Was the occurrence of this crop circle related to my frustration over the elusiveness of the phenomenon? . . . It did occur within 10-15 minutes of my having stated my disgust and it did occur in the closest growing plants . . . to my physical self. . . . Robbert and I, from our slightly different vantage points, were each quite convinced of both the intense power and the precision of the light "tubes"—both of us perceiving the incident as "deliberate, on purpose." . . . What are the chances that this recent amazing display was just coincidental? . . . Was there a consciousness in those light columns? Or, was there a consciousness directing them? . . . Robbert and I don't know. . . . What we hope is that 21st Century humanity will recognize this possibility soon and join in the effort to uncover new aspects of reality we may currently only faintly imagine.[30]

A Projection of Thought Patterns

Those who believe that human consciousness can form crop circles do not know the source of the power. Some believe it is a natural force contained within the human mind. Others say it is directed by God or extraterrestrials who use human consciousness as a tool. Crop circle expert Andy Thomas thinks the formations can be traced to what is called the collective unconscious. The term is used to describe thoughts buried deep in the subconscious—that is, thoughts that are common to all people. The thoughts of the collective unconscious are not in any single language but are made of common symbols, such as the Celtic cross and the yin/yang symbol that have existed for much of human history. These and other symbols are manifested by the collective unconscious in the form of crop circles. Thomas explains this concept:

> Some believe that crop circles are a projection of our thought patterns, manifesting when a critical mass of ideas overlap. At first the only concept enough of us shared was that of a circle. . . . Today, as mass media and the internet help build a global culture, the "circles" get exceedingly complex. This dynamic becomes amplified when people think about the crop circles themselves. Thinking about crop circles in a given area (like southern England) gives rise to more frequent and more elaborate crop circles in that area. . . . [There] is evidence that thought projection—either unconscious *or* conscious—causes [crop circles] to form. There are many stories and several documented cases of people concentrating on a given image and having it appear in the fields the following morning.[31]

As an example, Thomas cites the experience of pilot and crop circle photographer Busty Taylor. On one occasion, a prankster phoned Taylor and told him about a crop circle that had formed at a specific location. Although the circle did not exist, Taylor went in search of it, and after several sweeps over the area it appeared out of nowhere. Thomas believes Taylor manifested the crop circle with his thoughts because he had a strong desire to see it.

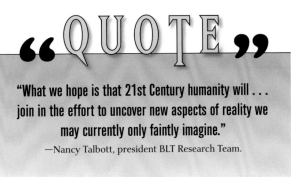

A Force of Nature

Since they first began multiplying in the late 1970s, crop circles have been attributed to angels, aliens, superhuman beings, and human brain power. They have even been blamed on mating hedgehogs that supposedly move in circles when reproducing, trampling down crops in unusual patterns. Those who reject the idea of animals or aliens continue to search for Earth energies that might be responsible. But even scientists who witness crop circles forming before their eyes cannot explain exactly what is causing them. Like the wind, the rain, and the weather, crop circles appear to be a force of nature—one that seems to be beyond human control.

CHAPTER 3

Circles from Space

On a hot, sunny July afternoon in 2005, Andrew Fowlds saw a bright ball of light appear in the sky over the Medway River Valley in Kent, England. The object, which he said "shone brilliantly like a star,"[32] was obviously not an airplane, helicopter, or balloon. Fowlds began following the light in his car, stopping occasionally to take photos of the distant white orb tracking across the clear blue sky.

Fowlds was familiar with crop circles. As a member of Medway Crop Circle Research (MCCR) he knew that two crop circles had appeared in the region in the last two months. Fowlds reported the lights to MCCR president Graham Tucker and showed him the photos. Both men believed the lights to be a harbinger of a crop circle appearance and they were right. At 7 A.M. the next morning an amazingly intricate crop circle was discovered near the village of Boxley, close to the area where Fowlds had seen the unusual light.

The Boxley formation was called a trefoil, a term that defines a design with three lobes or connected parts. The circle was about 200 feet (61m) across and appeared close to the busy M20 motorway. Tucker describes the Boxley Trefoil:

> [Right] at the centre of the formation stood an intriguing bunch of standing stems, that were manipulated in such a way as to effectively produce a standing figure with a crown of thorns! "The Circlemakers" had somehow twisted the top leaves of the plants into spike-like quills, which were quite sharp and pointed . . . and I mean sharp! As for the seedheads, they were bent at their base and allowed to droop downwards. . . . [This] design almost looks like some sort of face.[33]

Unearthly Balls of Light

Fowlds's experience was similar to that of hundreds of others who say they have seen unearthly balls of light, bright beams, or glowing orbs before extremely complex crop patterns appeared. Commenting on this phenomena, British Aerospace engineer Thomas Ray Dutton states that the circles are likely the work of UFOs: "It appears as though we are dealing with technology that is far superior to ours. Therefore we must assume that it is extraterrestrial in origin."[34]

Surprisingly, the first crop circle associated with UFOs was not found in southern England but thousands of miles away in Australia. On January 19, 1966, farmer George Pedley was driving his tractor on a sugar cane farm near Tully, Queensland. Pedley heard a loud noise, like air escaping from a blown tire. He suddenly saw a large, gray flying saucer spinning very fast, rising quickly from a nearby swamp. When he drove to the site to investigate, Pedley saw a round area, 30 feet (9.1m) in diameter, cleared in the swamp grass. The grass was flattened in clockwise curves to water level and the reeds were uprooted from the mud. The grass was not scorched, nor were the surrounding trees burned. Pedley noted the air smelled like sulfur but did not detect the odor of burning gasoline, which would be associated with a hay mower. Pedley later returned with a friend and took a series of photographs of what came to be known as the Tully saucer nest or Tully UFO nest.

Three Orbs of Light

The publicity surrounding the saucer nest soon attracted public attention. After more saucer nests appeared in the 1970s, Tully became known as Australia's UFO capital. By that time, crop circles were appearing with amazing regularity in southern England. Public interest was high, and on any given night, sky watchers could be found scanning the heavens over the region's many Neolithic monuments. One of those sky watchers, David Kingston, was a ufologist and former Royal Air Force pilot. Between 1957 and 1972 he had investigated numerous UFO reports made by pilots and other Air Force personnel. In the course of his work, Kingston saw several UFOs in the United Kingdom, the United States, and elsewhere.

On a warm summer night in 1976, Kingston was sitting with several other researchers on Clay Hill near Warminster when three separate orbs of colored light suddenly brightened the sky. During the next three hours, the globes wove around, sometimes joining into one globe and then separating again. Kingston picks up the story:

> [Suddenly] one of the orbs descended to some thirty feet above us and then flew down into a field at the base of Clay Hill. As dawn broke I noticed a flattened circle in a field of wheat. On inspection there were no broken stalks just a perfectly flattened circle some thirty feet in diameter. At that particular point in time I had seen and had knowledge of the famous "Tulley UFO Nests" in 1966 at Australia but had not heard of anything of a similar nature in this country.[35]

Light Bodies

Since the era of the Tully saucer nests and Clay Hill sighting, UFOs and crop circles have become firmly linked in the public mind. However, some crop circle researchers have come to dislike the term UFO when used to identify lights associated with crop circles. They say the term is technically correct, since the lights are unidentified flying objects. But UFOs are too closely associated with flying saucers and alien abductions. Most typical UFO reports describe spaceships shaped like discs, cigars, boomerangs, or triangles. These vehicles supposedly are as solid as airplanes and hover in the sky or zip around at impossible speeds. But ufologist Diahann Krishna believes the flying objects of light linked to crop circles are different than those in most UFO reports. Krishna says crop circle lights are not spaceships but bodies of light that travel through space. She prefers the ancient term *merkaba*, commonly used by New Age believers to define a powerful invisible energy force that can be generated by people when they meditate. According to Krishna, *merkaba* is also used by space aliens to visit Earth:

> The components of this name, mer-ka-ba, literally mean "light body" and it's known . . . as a vehicle that permits interdimensional travel. It is created by consciously rotating the electromagnetic fields around the body (any body including planets and atoms!). . . . As these fields rotate faster approaching the speed of light, a disc-like force-field is created which acts as a containment vessel for [space] beings to safely "step down" into our third dimensional world [to create crop circles].[36]

Merkaba lights are said to appear over ley lines and might not be seen by all who are present. The lights are also believed to respond to the thoughts of some observers, which might explain the dancing orbs and bright beams seen by Talbott and Van den Broeke in Hoeven in 2001. The power of the energy is such that aliens or others controlling the lights can create crop circles.

A Physical Communication

Skeptics say the *merkaba* theory is implausible. But ufologists point to an incident in Cache County, Utah, where it seemed as if orbs of light were being controlled by aliens. Cache County is an agricultural region about 85 miles (137km) north of Salt Lake City.

On August 23, 1996, a circle with a complex design appeared in Seth Alder's wheat field near Smithfield, Utah. The glyph featured a line 240 feet (73m) long with a large circle in the middle. The circle had what looked like straight handles attached to either side.

Alder, who was 81 years old, discovered the formation as he was harvesting the wheat. When he drove his tractor into the formation, the machine broke down. The farmer contacted the sheriff's department, and authorities sent an airplane over the formation to take photographs and shoot a video. Investigators determined the circle was made about a month earlier when the wheat stalks were still green. Although a deputy speculated it was created by gophers, the design was too complex to be generated by wild animals. Additionally, no signs of human or animal footprints were found around the formation. But as Alder told reporter Joshua B. Good from the *Salt Lake City Tribune:* "Well, you know, the scriptures tell of life on other planets. . . . Whoever or whatever did it spent some time on it. Unless it was a big machine that sat down on it."[37] Alder's neighbor Judy Cobia also speculated on the space alien theory, "It looks like the spaceship just landed out here."[38]

When David Rosenfeld of the Utah UFO organization UU-FOH heard about the crop circle, he wanted to investigate. After arriving at Alder's farm at dusk, Rosenfeld discovered that the farmer had harvested all the wheat around the glyph, and not much was left to see since the circle had been driven over repeatedly by a tractor. However, Rosenfeld, who was accompanied by his girlfriend, noticed about 20 small white lights, 1 to 3 inches (2.5 to 7.6cm) in diameter, moving around the circle area. The lights were only observable from a distance and would disappear when the couple tried to approach them. But Rosenfeld believes that the orbs behaved as if they were controlled by an intelligent being:

> [We] tried to catch one at one point, ganging up on it, trying to trap it between us, but the light would just disappear, or blink out when we got too close. We chased the lights anyway and tried to get closer, unsuccessfully, but with the impression that the lights were teasing us to try. Some would "fly" or float around us as if they were playing with us, or checking us out, buzzing overhead then zipping off into the distance. It seemed that they would circle the field then come in closer toward us, but if we got too close they would be gone instantly, like a bubble popping. They made no sound. We were running around the field like children, we were definitely having fun! Even though we didn't know what they were, or why they were there. . . . It was almost like a physical communication in some strange unknown way. A language or sharing of "feeling" that was quite comfortable.[39]

An Orange Ostrich Egg

Rosenfeld went back to the field the next night with a video camera, but the lights did not return. However, when he reported his experience to Talbott, she said it was the only report she knew of where witnesses had seen, interacted with, and photographed lights around crop circles. She also noted that it was the first time that the crop circle light phenomenon had been observed

"Just a Bunch of Vandals"

In June 2004, a roughly 100-foot (30m) in diameter crop circle appeared in Spanish Fork, Utah. Some witnesses were amazed when they saw unusual balls of light they called UFOs. However, the farmer who owned the field where the circle appeared was unhappy with the developments, according to the following story from the *Provo Daily Herald:*

> A few south Spanish Fork residents awoke to an unfamiliar sight Monday morning when a mysterious crop circle appeared in a wheat field just off Main Street. . . . The circle appeared in one of

in the United States. That would change, however, when several eyewitnesses came forward after visiting the Spanish Fork, Utah, crop circle on June 27, 2004.

the fields owned by farmer Paul A. Prior of Springville. Prior was informed of the uncommon landmark Monday morning and was not pleased with the damage caused to his crops. "It was just a bunch of vandals doing some damage," Prior said. "I wish they wouldn't trespass, and I wish they would do their art somewhere else." Prior estimated the damage to his crops was at least $300. He said he thinks the crop circle was created by local kids or other people not quite in their right minds.

Todd Hollingshead, "Spanish Fork Field Takes on Uncommon Characteristic," *Daily Herald*, June 29, 2004. www.harktheherald.com.

The Spanish Fork formation, carved into a barley field, consisted of one large outer ring with an inner ring that looked something like a crude drawing of an eyeball. This was adorned with

2 smaller rings outside the main formation, connected by straight paths that ran through the eyeball. A week after the formation appeared, a fourth circle was mysteriously added to the original design. The entire glyph measured 207 feet by 118 feet (63m by 36m).

Crop circle researcher Linda Moulton Howe interviewed a family that lived about 6 miles (9.6km) from the crop circle. They wished to remain anonymous but claimed to have seen mysterious white lights dancing over the area on July 3, before the final glyph appeared.

The family—a mother, father, son, and daughter—were driving by the Spanish Fork formation at 11:30 P.M. looking for signs of pranksters carving glyphs into the fields. When they arrived at the formation they saw 15 or 20 little golf ball-size lights with tails moving around over the design. The light motions were squiggly and curly, and they danced like those seen by Rosenfeld. But according to the mother, when they tried to take pictures, odd events ensued:

> [What] is really weird is that we took 26 or 27 pictures and we had a digital camera. We were taking pictures and we got to the end of it when we had a whole bunch of them . . . the camera started self-deleting and we had to turn the camera off to save [the remaining pictures]. We had nearly 30 pictures and we ended up with 12 because that's how fast they were self-deleting.[40]

The family left, but the mother and daughter were so intrigued with the crop circle they returned several hours later. By this time the lights seemed to have formed into strange orange orbs. According to the mother, "I looked over and there was this orange thing that was like an ostrich egg tipped to its side and it was floating to the side of us (as we were driving in the car). I noticed it for a few seconds. . . . [It was] the color of a glowing coal."[41] As the daughter tried to take photographs, the car began behaving in a bizarre manner. The battery warning signal lit up, and the car's lights repeatedly dimmed and got brighter. Then the automatic door locks opened and closed over and over. As suddenly as it appeared, the orange orb disappeared, and the car's electrical system returned to normal. As with Rosenfeld's experience, the people in the car believed the light was playing with them. As the mother said, "I was driving and I had my foot to the floor, but my car wouldn't go more than 35 mph. Then when the thing got ahead of us and flew away, it was only a matter of seconds I was going 65 mph because my foot was still floored to the gas. It was like, 'I've played enough. Now, I'm leaving.'"[42]

UFO Tracks

Thousands of people have witnessed odd illuminations before or during crop circle formation. But this is not the only odd event that has been reported immediately before the appearance of crop circles. On June 21, 2005, Mike Booth was pedaling his bicycle through an area called Boreham Down near Alton Barnes, Wiltshire. As the sun was setting Booth looked up to see four white metallic, dome-shaped objects gliding over a nearby wheat field. Booth stopped to watch and then noticed that the mysterious objects had left flattened tracks behind.

As with the encounters in Utah, the flying domes seemed to

"It looks like the spaceship just landed out here."

—Judy Cobia, farmer, speculating on the source of a Utah crop circle.

*Opposite:
Witnesses
have described
bright lights
and large,
orange spheres
(similar to the
one pictured
here) illumi-
nating fields
immediately
before crop
circles appear
and even while
they are form-
ing. One such
report surfaced
in Utah in
2004.*

sense that someone was watching them at work. In this case, the domes stopped moving completely. Booth seemed to understand what was happening and decided he should leave. He was soon pedaling his bike toward Alton Barnes. However, Booth returned to the field the next day and took pictures of the wide, flattened trails purportedly left by the UFOs. Although Booth could not see it from his position on the road, the tracks led over a hill to an intricate geometric formation with 21 major parts. Because the region is regularly patrolled by crop circle researchers in airplanes, researchers assumed that the formation was not there the day before or it would have been reported.

Besides Booth's report of UFOs in the area, the crop circle was unusual for another reason. Most designs consist of flattened, but not broken, plants. But the outer perimeter of the large Boreham Down formation was made from wheat that had been shredded into small pieces. The rest of the formation had flattened plants, but the border looked as if it had been created by a gigantic lawn-mower. The farmer who owned the field denied making the design with his harvesting equipment, leaving researchers mystified.

Another Enigma

Six weeks after the Boreham Down formation appeared, Belgian crop circle investigator Tommy Borms visited the site. Borms discovered that the tracks Booth had seen being created by flying objects were unusual. The wheat stalks had been flattened from the edges of the track to the middle. Those in the center were left in standing clumps like a Mohawk-style haircut. Borms also discovered that the nodes on the stems were lengthened in an unusual manner. While elongated nodes are commonly seen in crop circles, these nodes were stretched longer than any

previously observed. As with the shredded wheat, researchers did not understand why the nodes in the tracks were lengthened while those in the main design were not.

Another strange incident occurred over the Boreham formation on August 8, nearly seven weeks after it appeared. The site was being explored by French ufologist Pierre Beake and his wife. Beake had been photographing light orbs and UFOs around the world for several decades. During some of his photographic expeditions Beake saw nothing unusual with the naked eye. But when he developed the pictures, light phenomena and traditional types of UFOs were seen in the photographs.

When Beake and his wife began taking pictures at the Boreham Down site around 4:30 P.M., they did not see anything peculiar. But when they checked the digital camera, one of the photographs clearly showed a shiny metallic UFO. Beake had seen similar objects near Nice, France, where he had been taking photographs since the mid-1970s. However, no crop circles were ever reported at the French site. After Talbott examined Beake's photograph, she wrote: "This is the first, clear, daytime photograph of what looks like a relatively close UFO in the middle of the world's most active crop circle environment. Whether it has anything at all to do with the circles is unknown and why it was not visible to the eye, but only to the camera, is another enigma."[43]

Forming in Front of the Camera

The UFO photo from Boreham Down attracted the attention of ufologist Winston Keech, who had been exploring the Alton Barnes region for two decades. Keech wanted to shoot pictures and videos of crop circles being formed, and in recent years he assembled a number of expensive, high-tech cameras. Among them was an infrared closed-circuit television (CCTV) camera, a type of video recorder used for nighttime surveillance at banks, casinos, airports, and military installations. When Keech conducted a sky watch at Alton Barnes on July 7, 2007, he set up the CCTV along with four other cameras.

As Keech's cameras rolled, a mega-crop circle seemed to appear out of a sheet of light. The pattern was massive, over 1,000 feet (305m) long and 520 (158.5) feet wide, with over 90 separate circles within the formation and 60 surrounding the main design. Keech describes what took place:

> [What] is most remarkable is that it is absolutely known to have been formed within 1 hour 45 minutes and that it was filmed forming by five separate cameras (including infrared CCTV) and in the presence of three witnesses which is unprecedented. To the naked eye, observers saw only a white flash similar to sheet lightning at 3:13 A.M. But the ultra low light CCTV camera, pointed at the field, saw considerably more. Viewing the lighting enhanced video, over the following seven minutes, the circle would seem . . . to develop into the full formation in front of the camera.[44]

Several UFO reports were filed in the region after the circle was created, and Keech is convinced that aliens were at work in the fields that night.

A Bunch of Geeks

Most witnesses to UFO-related crop circles assume the circle makers are aliens. But ever since Levengood determined that plants in crop formations were bent by a brief, high-heat process, conspiracy theorists have speculated that the military might be responsible for crop circles. These people believe the unidentified flying objects over the fields are top-secret satellites. Controlled by military personnel on Earth, the satellites use high-tech laser cannons, or masers, to make intricate patterns in the fields. Masers were first developed in the United States in the 1950s. Since that time they have been adapted to warfare, shooting microwave radiation to disrupt enemy communications. Some speculate about the existence of similar weapons that can kill enemy troops on the battlefield.

Conspiracy theorists believe that the U.S. military, working with Great Britain, create crop circles in order to test the power and accuracy of the laser cannons. To cover their tracks, the government agencies plant stories about aliens in the press or use secret agents to say they witnessed UFOs making crop circles.

Those who support the military microwave theory point out that microwave radiation is known to cause various problems reported by circle investigators. These include irregular compass behavior, electrical equipment disturbances, crackling sounds, and animals acting oddly. Feelings of euphoria or sickness among witnesses are blamed on fumes that are created when fertilizers or pesticides are burned by microwaves. George Anthony Paniagua, who has studied masers and crop circles, makes his case for U.S. military involvement:

Visitors stand inside one of the massive circles that mysteriously appeared at Alton Barnes in Wiltshire, England, in July 2007. Witnesses said the pattern appeared suddenly, seemingly out of a bright flash of light.

Conspiracy theorists
say the U.S. military
makes intricate
patterns in fields to
test the power and
accuracy of high-tech
laser cannons.

[Maser] technology is used by a military satellite in order to "shoot" maser beams at precisely computed locations on our planet. This kind of satellite is aimed to destroy anything at any time at any location under any atmospheric circumstances. Such a satellite is not publicly known, i.e. kept secret, of course. . . . It is all in the game of cover-up, misusing the belief of mankind that extraterrestrials are having an artistic party overnight. . . . [By] aiming a computer guided maser at high altitude towards a crop field, in about 15 seconds a large complex pattern can be projected and "cooked in" using rotating maser beams. . . . Once again, crop circles are NOT made by Aliens or UFOs, but simply by a maser satellite, programmed by a bunch of geeks.[45]

Messages from an Advanced Society

As with most theories concerning crop circles, an alternative to the maser satellite hypothesis has been proposed. And this one points to space aliens. Crop circle specialist Tom Sutter believes that the formations are created by aliens who are using a microwave device called a magnetron. This machine forces electrons through a magnetic field which makes them spin in such a way that they create microwave energy.

When aimed at a plant, the alien version of the magnetron causes water molecules to split apart into their hydrogen and oxygen components. These atoms become highly agitated and rejoin over and over, creating energy which feeds back into the magnetron. Sutter believes that this process can create an endless energy supply. He thinks aliens are using magnetrons to

One expert believes that space aliens have used magnetrons to create crop circles. A magnetron, pictured here during testing in a research lab, is a device that creates microwave radiation for use in treating cancerous tumors.

create crop circles in order to demonstrate their energy device to humanity: "Bluntly, [aliens] are telling us that our primary means of creating needed energies, namely oil, ain't quite the way. . . . Let's assume that YOU were a member of an advanced society and wanted to convey to a lesser advanced society—the concept of the [magnetron]. How would YOU go about doing that via bending crops?"[46]

While Sutter believes that crop circles are an energy tutorial made by an advanced society of aliens, skeptics point out that magnetrons are already in use. They have been installed in every microwave oven ever sold. Sutter counters that the aliens are demonstrating an overlooked way to utilize microwaves that would allow society to wean itself from oil.

In the final analysis, Sutter's theory is no more far-fetched than any other concerning crop circle formations. For some, it seems unlikely that space aliens would travel all the way to Earth only to draw pretty patterns in English wheat fields. This leads them to conclude that ETs must be trying to communicate an important message to earthlings. On the other hand, conspiracy theorists know that the military has a long history of developing secret weapons that are mistaken for UFOs when eyewitnesses see them at work. For these people, shadowy government forces are behind nearly every unexplained mystery.

Whatever their source, crop circles are at once puzzling, magical, and controversial. The reasons for the formation phenomena seem beyond human reach. The truth is as elusive as the buzzing lights dancing brightly over the fields.

CHAPTER 4

Hoaxers and Jokesters

On a warm July evening in 1976, artists Doug Bower and Dave Chorley sat at their customary corner table in the Percy Hobbs pub near Cheesefoot Head. After a while the 2 men, both in their early fifties, walked into a nearby wheat field to study the lay of the land. Bower recalled how he became interested in UFOs after reading a story about the Tully saucer nest when he lived in Australia in 1966. Then Bower pointed into the wheat field and said to Chorley, "What do you think would happen if we put a nest over there? People would think a flying saucer had landed."[47]

Chorley thought it was a great idea. The following week, after their usual visit to the pub, the two men walked out into the Devil's Punchbowl. Bower carried an iron bar about 5 feet (1.5m) long. As Chorley held one end of the bar in place, Bower swept it around in a circle. After that was accomplished, the men crawled

Cereologist Colin
Andrews believes
80 percent of
all crop circles
are human-made
while the other 20
percent are made by
unknown forces.

around the outer edge of the circle holding the bar between them. As they moved through the wheat, the plants were pushed down at a 90 degree angle in a flat swirl. Within 30 minutes, Bower and Chorley had completed their work; they had created a crop circle about 30 feet (9m) in diameter.

Planks and Ropes

Elated with the results, Bower and Chorley decided to continue their work. That summer they made 12 more circles, some as large as 80 feet (24m) across. The following year, they repeated the exercise, making a few circles every month. For 2 more years, Bower and Chorley made crop circles in the fields around Cheesefoot Head. While the 2 men became expert at flattening the wheat and barley into intriguing patterns, no one seemed to notice their handiwork. Chorley wanted to stop, but Bower promised him that one day their crop circles would attract large crowds. Chorley agreed to continue making the circles. But he believed a new method was needed because the iron bar required too much labor, and it was destroying the crops as well. In the summer of 1980, they switched to planks about 4 feet (1.2m) long, tied with ropes at each end. This new technique allowed them to walk upright while holding the planks beneath their feet. With each step, they pushed down a 4-foot-wide path (1.2m) through the field. The planks were light and allowed them to work faster and for longer periods. With a new plant-flattening method perfected, the men made another decision. They would choose the sites for their crop circles more carefully, finding fields that people would be more likely to see and that had some connection to UFO sightings.

For their first new site, the circle makers chose a field beneath the Westbury White Horse near Warminster. The White Horse is an unusual piece of art, a giant mound in the shape of a horse thought to have been carved from local chalk sometime in the late 1600s—or possibly earlier. The site was a popular picnic area, and it was also associated with UFO sightings. In May 1980, when Bower and Chorley made a circle formation in the oat field beneath the White Horse, they finally attracted the attention they had been hoping for. An article about the crop circle appeared in the *Wiltshire Times*, and it was picked up by a London tabloid. The papers did not identify the formation as human-made, leaving readers to speculate about the mysterious source of the circles.

In the years that followed, the circle makers learned to make more intricate patterns with multiple circles. Their most repeated pattern, one large circle surrounded by four smaller ones, was devised, according to Bower, "to make it look like a four-legged space ship had landed."[48]

A Grand Old Time

In the early 1980s dozens of crop circles anonymously made by Bower and Chorley were reported as having been made by swirling electronic vortices, UFOs, military lasers, and lovesick hedgehogs. The two men were thrilled when Delgado said the circles were made by creatures with a higher intelligence. However, the circle makers were bothered by Meaden's theory that natural forces, such as whirlwinds, were making the formations. This led Bower and Chorley to make the first ringed crop circle at Cheesefoot Head. To baffle the scientist, they flattened the grasses in a clockwise pattern in the inner circle. In the outer ring the plants were pushed down in a counter-clockwise fashion. Meaden was forced to admit that the formation could not possibly

Did You Know?

Doug Bower and Dave Chorley made their first crop circle in 1976.

A white horse carved hundreds of years ago from natural chalk on Wiltshire's Westbury Hill has attracted circle makers over the years. A more recent horse carving at nearby Roundway Hill (pictured, opposite page) has also been a popular site for crop circles.

have been created by wind vortices.

Bower and Chorley continued to develop more complex patterns. This not only fooled the experts but attracted a record number of tourists to the crop circles. Schnabel describes the joy the hoaxers experienced at such scenes:

> Sometimes Doug and Dave would go out on weekend afternoons themselves, to admire their works in the light of day, and mingle with the crowds, and feign innocence, asking people what they thought was making the circles, biting their tongues to keep from laughing at the answers. Eventually they became regulars around Cheesefoot Head, and became well known to Delgado and Andrews . . . to whom they were merely two old-timers enthusiastic about crop circles. . . . Oh yes, Doug and Dave had a grand old time.[49]

We Have Been Conned

By the late 1980s other circle makers had arrived on the scene. To keep their circles at the forefront, Bower created new designs that could not be imitated. His first was a series of triangles and rectangles based on abstract paintings from the 1920s. Next came the bug designs that came to be known as insectograms.

As the complexity of the patterns increased, so too did the wild theories devised to explain them. But after 13 years of tramping through fields in the dead of night, Bower, 67, and Chorley, 62, were getting tired of their prank. On September 3, 1991, Bower called reporter Graham Brough at the *Today* newspaper and confessed. To prove the truth of their story, he informed Brough

that they would make an insectogram the following weekend. He gave the reporter the location and showed him a drawing of the formation they would create.

Brough was convinced after the insectogram appeared at Sevenoaks as promised. *Today* ran a story exposing the hoaxers to the world. Doug and Dave, as they became known, received interview requests from reporters in the United States, Italy, Canada, and Germany.

Before the story broke, Bower contacted Delgado to warn him of what was to come. The crop circle expert who had sold thousands of books about supernatural forces at work said it was the worst day of his life. As Delgado told *Today:* "We have all been conned. Thousands of lives are going to be wrecked over this. The mystery of the circles—which has baffled experts for more than a decade—is today exposed as nothing more than a hoax by two artists."[50]

Bower and Chorley's confession did not convince all crop circle researchers. It was pointed out that their demonstration for the reporter left broken stalks and trampled wheat, unlike the cleanly bent stalks seen in other circles. Despite their detractors, Bower and Chorley took credit for creating as many as 250 crop circles.

Chorley died from cancer in 1997. Two years later, Bower appeared on a BBC television show to demonstrate how he had made crop circles with his old friend. Thinking back on his glory days as the world's most mysterious hoaxer, Bower recalled magical nights in the fields:

> [It] was just pure enjoyment on those beautiful summer nights for two artistic people under the stars amid all those cornfields. We were both 19th

Century people really. We were in another world. I don't consider being on a planet for 60 years is much use if you don't leave your mark. We didn't want to make publicity. We just wanted to make fools of the experts who were springing up everywhere. . . . Other people made money out of the [crop] circles . . . but all Dave and I got was a really big laugh. But its been a wonderful experience and I wouldn't have missed it for the world.[51]

Crop Conspiracies

Bower and Chorley's admission did little to stop the excitement that built up over the crop circle phenomenon. Hundreds of farmers made money by charging people admission to their fields where crop circles had appeared. In addition, dozens of books and hundreds of newspaper articles were published about the formations. With public attention largely focused on the crop circle mystery, many were unwilling to accept the simple truth that two aging men with too much time on their hands had created the frenzy.

Plus, crop circles continued to appear, some of them outside England, after Bower and Chorley faded from the headlines. Many were obvious hoaxes, as Andrews points out: "I concluded that 80 percent of all crop circles we investigated in England from 1999 through the year 2000 were manmade. This was one of the most important research findings to date because it cut to what was truly important: *the remaining 20 percent of the crop circles showed no sign of human hands.*"[52]

While even true believers had to admit that some circles were human-made, unusual events associated with crop circles

Insect-shaped crop circles of the 1990s, called insectograms, may have influenced later, more elaborate formations such as this dragonfly crop circle that appeared in a barley field near the village of Yatesbury, England, in June 2009.

continued. Light orbs were reported, and people continued to experience mental and physical effects within the crop circles. Cereologists also point to Levengood's studies that showed abnormalities in the wheat stalks, seeds, and soil taken from formations. As crop circle enthusiast Michael Chorost states, "The work of . . .

Levengood points to a cause which pumps energy into the plants, leaving them intact but causing damage within. This kind of damage is almost impossible to cause by [pranksters trampling on crops]."[53]

Crop circle conspiracy theorists have also weighed in on the hoax issue. In the conspiracy community, Bower, Chorley, and others who continued their work are accused of providing cover for the military. As Dehlinger writes: "In 1991 . . . the CIA and the British Ministry of Defense secretly persuaded two retired gentlemen, David Chorley and Douglas Bower, to declare that they were the authors of the crop circles that had been observed to date, without providing evidence to support their statement."[54]

Juvenile Behavior

The idea that the CIA paid the dodgy duo of Bower and Chorley to claim credit for crop circles seems unlikely. However, many who made money off the circles were deeply opposed to researchers who said the formations were human-made. Rosemary Ellen Guiley, a paranormal researcher who has written over 40 books on supernatural and mystical phenomena, learned this after concluding crop circles were made by hoaxers. In 1994 Guiley described the reaction of cereologists in *Fate* magazine:

> Charges fly back and forth that various people are guilty of hoarding data, passing misinformation or disinformation, exploiting circles for money, or of being CIA agents. I myself have been falsely accused of being a CIA agent, and of setting up an organization to pass disinformation. That anyone could believe such nonsense seemed preposter-

ous, but this libel has been passed around with seriousness. The juvenile behavior I have encountered astonishes me. In all the years I have spent working in the paranormal . . . I have never experienced anything such as I have found on the part of some cereologists. People who call themselves vampires have behaved with more decency than some of those with whom I have dealt in this field. . . . To attempt to discredit opposition by smearing it as evil is the stuff of cults and inquisitions. In both of those, there is no room for free thinking, for making up one's own mind.[55]

Andrews, who was a leading crop circle expert had similar experiences. After he appeared on radio and television to announce that 80 percent of crop circles were human-made, he says he was treated to: "Hate mail. Threats. Red-faced zealots screaming in my face. Contempt. Media ridicule. Professional scorn. Hatred. Insults."[56] Andrews was also accused of working for the CIA. But he points out that his statement was misunderstood. Many mistakenly think he said all crop circles were hoaxes, when what he did say is that 8 out of 10 were the work of pranksters. Andrews continues to believe the other 20 percent are "mysterious, unexplainable . . . [and] a gift to mankind."[57]

The Circlemakers

It is doubtful that the controversy over crop circles will soon diminish. Those who believe the formations are supernatural in origin will continue to clash with people like John Lundberg, an English artist and filmmaker. Lundberg founded a group called

Circlemakers in the early 1990s. The original goal of the arts group was to create large and elaborate crop circles that seemed as if they were made by otherworldly sources. Lundberg writes that he was driven to start the Circlemakers because he has a "deep interest in how myth and artifice [deception] can shape and alter reality."[58]

Lundberg has proved that peoples' reality can be shaped by tricks and fables. Although Circlemakers has created dozens of crop circles, some researchers continue to believe the formations were made by UFOs, supernatural Earth energies, or other mythical entities. On the Circlemakers Web site, Lundberg explains how the deceptions by pranksters have shaped the crop circle debate:

> For over 12 years [Bower and Chorley's] simple circle sets attracted the interest of scientists world-wide. During this time other artists began to emulate them, eventually superseding them, and continued a chain reaction—mutating from the UFO lore from which it still . . . nourishes—to become what is arguably the most mysterious . . . "paranormal" phenomenon this century. . . . [The] circles have become signs and portents of our time.[59]

The Circlemakers create most glyphs in secret, and the group does not openly take credit for its work. However, Lundberg joyfully admits to fooling experts into making cryptic pronouncements about formations made by the Circlemakers. In a 1993 case, the Circlemakers say they sprinkled powdered iron filings

around the center of the Nautilus formation in Yatesbury. The iron was collected by crop circle researchers and sent to Levengood, who analyzed the material. He concluded that the dust was from meteors. However, the Circlemaker Web site features a photograph of the canister that it says contained the iron filings. For his part, Levengood does not believe the iron was distributed by humans because of the way the particles were fused in the iron oxide mixture.

Lundberg's antics irked Andrews so much that he spent a great deal of money on private detectives to place the Circlemakers under surveillance. After the detectives filmed the group creating crop circles in 1994, Andrews was forced to admit, "These individuals were monitored and there is no doubt that they created some extremely complex and beautiful designs."[60]

A Beginner's Guide

While researchers like Andrews are very serious about their beliefs, the Circlemakers have a playful attitude about their work. They even encourage anonymous artists to make their own formations, and Lundberg has published a "Beginner's Guide" to instruct novices on crop circle creation. The guide instructs aspiring crop circle artists to create elaborate patterns on a computer. To make the circle they need simple tools such as a plastic garden roller, a 3- to 7-foot board (1 to 2m), or stalk-stomper, and a sturdy 100-foot tape measure (30.5m) like those used by land surveyors. The use of flashlights to read drawings and diagrams is discouraged because the lights might tip off sky watchers looking for UFOs.

When making circles, the pranksters are instructed to pay attention to established ley lines so cereologists can later attribute cosmic meaning to the designs. Lundberg provides a humorous description of the physical effects people might experience if the circles are not properly placed along ley lines:

> If the formation is situated contra-directionally to the flow of energy, this may result in . . . headaches, nausea, temporary limb-paralysis, aching

Sightseers visit a crop circle that mysteriously appeared in a northern California wheat field in 2003. Crops circles have been spotted in other parts of the United States and in Canada, Central and South America, France, Australia, Russia, Africa, and Japan.

joints, mental illness, deadly-orgone-radiation (DOR) exposure, demonic visions, negative abduction scenarios (memory loss, implant scarring, sore or bleeding . . . navels, and genitals, etc), and general disillusionment.[61]

The methods used to create crop circles are a little different than the techniques developed by earlier hoaxers. Teams of up to 10 people work together from a central point. A tape measure is used to provide an even radius to the edge of the formation, and stalk-stompers and garden rollers are used to push down the plants.

If the glyph artists do not leave any litter behind, such as cigarette butts and beer bottles, the formations are often judged genuine. This is especially true if the circle represents a shape associated with important subjects such as global warming, Eastern mysticism, computers, or space travel. Mysterious goo, such as petroleum jelly diluted in vodka can be left behind to fool experts. And truly creative people can go near the site the night before and create a light show with lasers, spotlights, or powerful flashlights, providing they do not get caught. The effectiveness of these techniques has been demonstrated repeatedly. In at least a dozen cases, crop circle experts pronounced that a formation was genuine only to have the Circlemakers prove them wrong by producing a videotape of artists creating the glyph.

Spare Stars and Shredded Wheat

Most of the work conducted by the Circlemakers is anonymous. But to raise funds to continue their work, the group has created crop circles for businesses wishing to promote their products in an entirely new way. The first such effort took place in August 1998 when the Circlemakers created an advertisement for a Mitsubishi car called the Space Star. The design was quite large, 350 feet by 110 feet (106.7m by 33.5m), and took a team of three artists 12 hours to complete.

By agreeing to produce the ad, the Circlemakers generated a great deal of controversy. Anonymous callers threatened to sabotage the formation. While the work was being carried out, a group of cereologists surrounded the field to heckle the crop artists. The company producing the ad was forced to hire security guards to prevent angry "croppies," as Lundberg calls them, from entering the fields and stopping work. The effort paid off, however, as the ad generated intense interest. The morning after it was completed, the area was filled with researchers, tourists, journalists, and TV crews. The carnival-like atmosphere was heightened by actors, hired by Mitsubishi, who impersonated "Men in Black" secret service agents pretending to hunt for space aliens.

Two years later the group used lawnmowers to carve the words "Do the Dew" into a field of barley in Washington State for Mountain Dew. In 2005 the Circlemakers created formations in other parts of the United States to promote Microsoft's X-Box 360 game console. For this promotion the group made designs in the sandy beaches of Florida and California and mowed a formation into the grass in a field in Oklahoma. The work was filmed for a crop circle documentary shown on MTV.

Perhaps the most inspired piece of creative marketing was the "100% whole grain crop circle"[62] the group made for Shredded Wheat. The formation was drawn out on 18 diagrams. It took 4 circle artists 14 hours to complete. The finished formation, with

Suspicious Behavior

Doug Bower had been making crop circles with Dave Chorley for seven years before anyone knew about their anonymous pranks. However, Bower's wife Ilene became very suspicious about her husband's behavior several years before the public found out about the hoax. Bower was coming home very late on weekend nights and seemed unusually happy. Ilene thought her husband was seeing another woman and began to keep track of the mileage running up on their car's odometer. After seeing that Bower was driving much farther than

the words "Shredded Wheat" inside a heart, was created on a Hertfordshire farm that supplies wheat to the company that makes the cereal. Pictures of the finished work were used on cereal boxes.

Not all public Circlemakers work is commercial. In 2007 the group traveled to Mexico with the environmental group Green-the local pub on the weekends, Ilene confronted him. Bower understood he had to inform Ilene of his long-running prank. He dumped out a pile of photographs and newspaper clippings, along with the original drawings he made of the crop circles. When that failed to mollify Ilene, Bower showed her the planks, ropes, and other equipment he used to make crop circles. Ilene did not believe any of it. Finally, after swearing her to secrecy, Bower took her along on one of his Friday night circle-making missions with Chorley. When the circle showed up in the local newspaper on Sunday, Ilene was finally convinced that it was the love of art and practical jokes, not another woman, that was keeping her husband up late at night.

peace to make a political statement in the corn. Greenpeace has been waging a campaign against genetically engineered food since the 1990s. In Mexico genetically engineered corn pollen, carried on the winds, has intermixed with traditional, organic corn growing in the fields. To raise awareness about the genetically engineered corn contamination, Greenpeace engaged the

Circlemakers to create a 200-foot circle (61m) with a giant question mark in the center. It was extremely difficult work. The crop artists were faced with tropical heat and had to manipulate corn plants 8 feet (2.4m) tall. But the work was featured in 3 Mexican newspapers and attracted national attention to the problem.

The commercial activities of the Circlemakers are considered evil by those who believe crop circles are mystical objects. Consequently, Lundberg has received hundreds of threats including nasty emails. He says, "I'm a heretic. I'm attacking their belief system."[63] Critics like Andrews are particularly annoyed by the Circlemakers, commenting, "I wish John and his band of merry men would just disappear."[64]

Weird Things Happen

While the Circlemakers annoy cereologists, even they admit that weird things happen while they are laying down crops in the fields. One team of Circlemakers, led by Julian Richardson, had an unusual experience while creating a complicated design during a dark summer night in 1992. After turning a complex, mathematical drawing into reality, Richardson writes,

> Suddenly my attention was drawn to a light that had appeared from nowhere. It was a few hundred yards away and directly in front of us. As soon as I'd registered its presence I alerted my colleagues. Amazed, we stood there gazing at this football-sized orange light as it hung motionless, about forty feet above the surrounding countryside. After an estimated five seconds the light began to

slowly descend. Within another five seconds it had descended about ten feet and had faded into invisibility. With little time to spare, we excitedly returned to our work, always hopeful of a repeat performance. Subsequent daylight checks revealed no evidence of the light's existence. . . . Did we witness a naturally occurring phenomenon—or were we really being scanned by the genuine circlemakers?[65]

Lundberg has also seen what he calls alien lightforms while making crop circles in Wiltshire: "[We] did see a classic UFO—a dark, silent, cigar-shaped craft with tiny strobe lights at each end. . . . Four of us witnessed it as it slowly arced across a clear starlit sky."[66] Such sightings connect the Circlemakers to those who believe supernatural forces are at work. As Lundberg writes: "Our work . . . can sometimes act to catalyze a wide range of paranormal events. I . . . believe there is a genuine [mystical] phenomenon . . . [and] we're a part of it."[67]

Community and Controversy

The mystical forces crop circle artists feel when they are at work is exhibited in various ways. A few argue that the designs that come to them in their thoughts, dreams, and daydreams are supernatural in origin. Some believe that even Bower and Chorley might have been doing the work of alien forces, driven to the fields by a higher power that guided their hands and feet. Whatever the case, the crop circles that have been created since the 1980s constitute some of the most beautiful public art ever created on a monumental scale. With nearly 10,000 formations appearing in recent decades, the works have been viewed by countless millions on TV and the Internet.

Perhaps the argument over whether the circles are made by humans is irrelevant. Outside of a small group of crop circle fanatics, the formations have created community and brought widespread joy to observers. This point is not lost on Circlemakers cofounder Rob Irving who calls the formations "temporary sacred sites."[68] This is based on Irving's observations that people react in spiritual and mystical ways when they enter crop circles. They sing, dance, meditate, and often experience feelings of extreme elation. Commenting on the importance of this phenomenon, circle researcher Mark Fussell writes, "People should pay attention to what goes on after the crop circles are made rather than focusing on what makes the crop circles."[69] Perhaps that is the secret to the circles that has long eluded experts. For whatever or whoever creates them, crop circles have certainly made a huge impression, captivating the public imagination, and creating controversy that continues to this day.

NOTES

Introduction: Mystery in the Meadows

1. Quoted in Brainsturbator, "Crop Circles 4: Into the Weird," March 6, 2007. www.brainsturbator.com.

2. Quoted in Keay Davidson, "Real Culprit Behind Crop Circles? Skeptics Point to the Media," *San Francisco Chronicle*, July 12, 2003. www.sfgate.com.

Chapter 1: Rings of Record

3. Quoted in *Daily Mail Online*, "Jellyfish, Dragonflies and Peace Symbols: The Summer of Crop Circles Is Just Getting Started," June 5, 2009. www.dailymail.co.uk.

4. Quoted in *Daily Telegraph*, "Dragonfly Crop Circle Appears in Wiltshire," June 4, 2009. www.telegraph.co.uk.

5. Quoted in William Andrews, ed., *Bygone Hertfordshire*. London: William Andrews, 1898, pp. 214-15.

6. Quoted in Andrews, *Bygone Hertfordshire*, p. 215.

7. Quoted in Farshores, "Flying Triangle Encounters," July 23, 1999. http: //farshores. org.

8. Quoted in The Mystery of Crop Circles, "The Mysterious Crop Formations," The Supernatural Zone, 2009. www.qsl.net.

9. Andy Thomas, "Vital Signs Extracts," Vital Signs, 2009. www.vitalsignspublishing.co.uk.

10. Quoted in Freddy Silva, *Secrets in the Fields.* Charlottesville, VA: Hampton Roads, 2002, p. 6.

11. Quoted in Robert Rickard and John Michell, *Unexplained Phenomena: A Rough Guide Special.* London: Rough Guides, 2000, p. 184.

12. Ralph Noyes, ed., *The Crop Circle Enigma.* Lower Lake, CA: Gateway, 1991, p. 18.

13. Noyes, *The Crop Circle Enigma*, p. 19.

14. Jim Schnabel, *Round in Circles*. Amherst, NY: Prometheus, 1994, p. 21.

15. Quoted in Schnabel, *Round in Circles*, p. 31.

16. Quoted in Schnabel, *Round in Circles*, p. 33.

17. Quoted in Noyes, *The Crop Circle Enigma*, p. 46.

18. Thomas, "Vital Signs Extracts."

19. Silva, *Secrets in the Fields*, p. 19.

20. Quoted in Silva, *Secrets in the Fields*, p. 20.

Chapter 2: Earth Energies

21. Judith Moore and Barbara Lamb, *Crop Circles Revealed*. Flagstaff, AZ: Light Technology, 2001, p. 9.

22. Quoted in Joe Nickell, *Real-Life X-Files*. Lexington: University Press of Kentucky, p. 71.

23. Quoted in Silva, *Secrets in the Fields*, p. 282.

24. Quoted in Silva, *Secrets in the Fields*, p. 283.

25. Quoted in Werner Anderhug and Hans Peter Roth, *Crop Circles*. New York: Lark, 2002, p. 107.

26. Quoted in Anderhug and Roth, *Crop Circles*, p. 111.

27. Quoted in Anderhug and Roth, *Crop Circles*, p. 111.

28. Quoted in Silva, *Secrets in the Fields*, p. 126.

29. Nancy Talbott, "Other Facts," BLT Research Team, 2009. www.bltresearch.com.

30. Nancy Talbott, "Eyewitness Report of Crop Circle Being Formed in the Netherlands," BLT Research Team, 2009. www.bltresearch.com.

31. Quoted in Alan Muskat, "Crop Circles: A Dream Come True," 2005. www.alanmuskat.com.

Chapter 3: Circles from Space

32. Andrew Fowlds, "'Ball of Light' Sighting, Medway Valley, Saturday, July 16th, 2005," Medway Crop Circle, 2006. www.medwaycropcircle.co.uk.

33. Graham Tucker, "Crop Circles of Kent of 2005," Medway Crop Circle, 2006. www.medwaycropcircle.co.uk.

34. Quoted in Anderhug and Roth, *Crop Circles*, p. 112.

35. David Kingston, "Former British Royal Air Force Official Saw Alien Orb Create Crop Circle," *Canadian*, July 29, 2009. www.agoracosmopolitan.com.

36. Diahann Krishna, "UFO Sighting in Cambridgeshire Crop Circle," Crop Circle Research, June 29, 2009.

37. Quoted in Aliendave, "Utah Crop Circles," July 12, 2004. www.aliendave.com.

38. Quoted in Aliendave, "Utah Crop Circles."

39. David Rosenfeld, "Crop Circle Light Phenomenon," Aliendave, 2005. www.aliendave.com.

40. Quoted in Linda Moulton Howe, "The 2004 Spanish Fork Cropcircle," Aliendave, 2004. www.aliendave.com.

41. Quoted in Howe, "The 2004 Spanish Fork Cropcircle."

42. Quoted in Howe, "The 2004 Spanish Fork Cropcircle."

43. Nancy Talbott, "Boreham Down UFO," Rense, June 22, 2006. www.rense.com.

44. Quoted in BBC Wiltshire, "Crop Circle Creation on Film," July 30, 2009. www.bbc.co.uk.

45. George Anthony Paniagua, "Crop Circles Made by Military Satellites," Watcher Files, 2009. www.sherryshriner.com.

46. Tom Sutter, "Are Crop Circles Free Energy Tutorials? Tom Sutter's Theory," CTRL, December 14, 2000. www.mail-archive.com.

Chapter 4: Hoaxers and Jokesters

47. Quoted in Schnabel, *Round in Circles*, p. 268.

48. Quoted in Schnabel, *Round in Circles*, p. 270.

49. Schnabel, *Round in Circles*, p. 272.

50. Quoted in UFO Era, "More on Dave & Doug, Elderly Circle 'Hoaxers'—with Ties to Top-Secret Pine Gap Spy Center in Australia!" 2009. www.ufoera.com.

51. Quoted in Manchester Features, "Confessions of a Crop Circle Con Man," August 2, 2009. www.manchester.com.

52. Colin Andrews, *Crop Circles: Signs of Contact*. Franklin Lakes, NJ: New Page, 2003, p. 15.

53. Quoted in Schnabel, *Round in Circles*, p. 278.

54. Emmanuel Dehlinger, "Crop Circles: Military Use of a Microwave Laser Beam Cannon," *Ovnis: l'armée démaskée*, August 30, 2007. www.ovnis.atfreeweb.com.

55. Rosemary Ellen Guiley, "Circular Madness: The Descent of Cereology," Rutgers University, January 12, 1994. http://paul.rutgers.edu.

56. Andrews, *Crop Circles: Signs of Contact*, p. 153.

57. Andrews, *Crop Circles: Signs of Contact*, p. 157.

58. John Lundberg, "About John Lundberg," Off Kilter, 2007. www.offkilter.co.uk.

59. John Lundberg, "Beginner's Guide," Circlemakers, 2007. www.circlemakers.org.

60. Quoted in Peter Carlson, "Fertile Imaginations," *Washington Post*, August 9, 2002. www.washingtonpost.com.

61. Lundberg, "Beginner's Guide."

62. John Lundberg, "Shredded Wheat," Circlemakers, 2007 www.circlemakers.org.

63. Quoted in Carlson, "Fertile Imaginations."

64. Quoted in Carlson, "Fertile Imaginations."

65. Julian Richardson, "Amber Gambler," Circlemakers, 2008. www.circlemakers.org.

66. Quoted in Carlson, "Fertile Imaginations."

67. John Lundberg, "Alien Light Forms," Circlemakers, 2007. www.circlemakers.org.

68. Quoted in Lundberg, "Alien Light Forms."

69. Quoted in Mary Carroll Nelson, *Crop Circles: An Art of Our Time.* Albuquerque: Fresco Fine Art, 2007, p. 17.

FOR FURTHER RESEARCH

Books

Steve Alexander and Karen Alexander, *Crop Circles: Signs, Wonders and Mysteries.* Edison, NJ: Chartwell, 2009. This book is filled with dozens of beautiful aerial photographs of recent crop circles. The authors do not try to explain who or what made the formations but explore them as a great mystical and fascinating art form.

Toney Allman, *Stonehenge.* San Diego: ReferencePoint, 2008. This book provides insight into the wonders of Stonehenge, the site of hundreds of crop circles. The author explores the mysteries associated with the ancient monument, including why it might have been built and who could have built it.

Gregory Branson-Trent, *Aliens Among Us: A History of Extraterrestrials, Crop Circles, Abductions and UFO's.* Scotts Valley, CA: CreateSpace, 2009. The author explores UFOs from their appearance in ancient cave paintings and scriptures to modern sightings and encounters near crop circles.

Michael Glickman, *Crop Circles: The Bones of God.* Berkeley, CA: Frog, 2009. The author, who has been studying English crop circles since 1990, explores their meanings, origins, and relationship to human spirituality.

Lucy Pringle, *Crop Circles: Art in the Landscape.* London: Frances Lincoln, 2007. The author has been taking photographs of English crop circles from helicopters and small airplanes since the mid-1990s. As one of the leading experts on crop circle phenomena Pringle explores the mysteries that continue to baffle scientists around the world.

Web Sites

BLT Research Team (www.bltresearch.com). The primary focus of the BLT Research Team is crop circle research, including the discovery, scientific documentation, and evaluation of physical changes induced in plants, soils, and other materials at crop circle sites. The Web site contains scientific papers, a USA crop circle list, and up-to-date reports and photos of the most recent formations.

Circlemakers (http://circlemakers. org). This Web site is maintained by a group of "cereal artists" who create large and elaborate crop circles meant to fool the experts. The site provides updates and photos of the Circlemakers' latest crop circle creations in addition to case histories, articles that challenge crop circle experts, and archives of past hoaxes.

Crop Circle Connector (www. cropcircleconnector.com). One of the most detailed sites about crop circles in England with an extensive gallery and archives, news of the latest circles, articles about crop circle research, and information about crop circle conferences.

Independent Crop Circle Researchers' Association (ICCRA) (www.iccra. org). The Web site run by the ICCRA features American crop circles and is designed to provide insight into their formation for researchers and the general public. The site features articles with investigative field reports, a historical archive of formations, and methods and tools used in researching crop circles in the fields.

The UK Crop Circle Team (UKCCT) (www.ukcropcircles.co.uk). Founders of the UKCCT are dedicated to studying the finer details of each crop circle formation from the ground level. The Web site analyzes crop circle locations and the experiences of visitors who enter the formations.

INDEX

ABOUT THE AUTHOR

Stuart A. Kallen is a prolific author who has written more than 250 nonfiction books for children and young adults over the past 20 years. His books have covered countless aspects of human history, culture, and science, from the building of the pyramids to the music of the twenty-first century. Some of his recent titles include *How Should the World Respond to Global Warming?*, *Romantic Art*, and *Communication with the Dead*. Kallen is also an accomplished singer-songwriter and guitarist in San Diego, California.